Spring Gatherings

Spring Gatherings

Casual Food to Enjoy with Family and Friends

Rick Rodgers

Photographs by Ben Fink

WILLIAM MORROW

An Imprint of HarperCollinsPublishers

HarperCollins books may be purchased for educational, business, or sales promotional use. For information please write: Special Markets Department, HarperCollins Publishers, 10 East 53rd Street, New York, NY 10022.

FIRST EDITION

Designed by Lorie Pagnozzi and Ashley Halsey

Library of Congress Cataloging-in-Publication Data
Rodgers, Rick, 1953–
    Spring Gatherings: casual food to enjoy with family and friends / Rick Rodgers;
photographs by Ben Fink. —1st ed.
        p.   cm.
    Includes index.
    ISBN 978-0-06-167251-4
    1. Cookery, American. 2. Menus. I. Title.
TX715.R7264 2010
641.5973—dc22

2009027391

10 11 12 13 14   OV/RRD   10 9 8 7 6 5 4 3 2 1

To my parents, who managed to make
March 21 more than just the first day of spring . . .

Acknowledgments

My name may be on the jacket, but there were many other people who lent their talents to creating this cookbook.

Thanks again to everyone at William Morrow for their unstinting support, not only with this book, but with our others over the years. David Sweeney got the *Seasonal Gatherings* series off the ground. Cassie Jones edited this book with aplomb, and her assistant, Jessica Deputato, kept track of endless details. I am especially beholden to designers Lorie Pagnozzi and Ashley Halsey and Mary Schuck of Morrow's art department for giving the book its distinctively beautiful look. And to Adam Rochkind and DeeDee DeBartolo for getting the word out. And I am grateful for the collaboration of Sonia Greenbaum, my copy editor.

Ben Fink did another batch of gorgeous photos. And thanks to his crew, Jamie Kimm, food stylist, and Roy Finamore, prop stylist, for pulling off the appetizing cover.

My home team consists of Susan Ginsburg, my invaluable friend and agent; her equally indispensable assistant, Bethany Strout; Diane Kniss, the "sister I never had," who doubles as my kitchen manager; Judy Epstein, who also is a great help in the kitchen; and Patrick Fisher, my in-house director of quality control and the handsomest dishwasher in the business.

Contents

Introduction

I grew up in Northern California, and most people assume that just because the seasonal changes there aren't as dramatic as those on the East Coast, there are no seasons at all. The shifts are more subtle, I grant you, but they do exist. Of all the seasons, I anticipated spring the most for many reasons. My birthday is March 21, the first full day of spring, so the season's start was duly marked with a slice of birthday cake. In spring, you could count on rains to turn the normally golden dry hills a fresh, verdant green, the better for hiking and bike riding. I would also see a shift in what was served on the table, and the foods were my favorites.

When strawberries would make their short appearance at the local farm stand, we would line up for the juicy red berries that would be sliced and sugared to top warm shortcake heaped with thick whipped cream. When asparagus and artichokes were abundant and cheap, we would devour an entire platter of them as a vegetarian Lent or meatless Friday dinner, accompanied by no more than lemon wedges and sourdough bread with butter. Our backyard apricot tree would bloom with countless white flowers that would eventually transform into golden fruit for pies and cobblers and eating out of hand. (In fact, I once ate so many that I took a break from them for a few years.) Neighbors would show up on the porch with offerings of peas from a too prolific vine or mint that had grown out of control, as mint tends to do.

The farm stand in our suburban town had a roster of produce that, of course, changed with the various growing cycles. Our farmer's plot wasn't big enough for staggered plantings, so the length of availability was determined by how much he could plant and harvest at once. There was no procrastination, as the supply was limited. When the strawberries were gone, you had to wait a year until the next harvest. This gave a simple dessert of strawberry-rhubarb pie special resonance. It was impressed upon me that its pleasures were fleeting, and to be savored.

This is different from the way we cook today, with produce available year-round. I could buy strawberries in January if I wanted to. But that doesn't mean they're worth eating. If I want juice-filled, sweet, delicate berries that remind me of the berries of my youth, I still have to wait for their annual springtime appearance.

When I moved to the East Coast, I discovered a new group of seasonal spring bounty. Tightly curled fiddleheads and sorrel were eagerly anticipated. Some items, such as Vidalia onions, Key limes, green garlic, ramps, and garlic shoots, which were formerly regional specialties, were added to the list as they became more readily available.

Back home, springtime holidays meant gathering with loved ones for meals that were out of the ordinary—sumptuous roast lamb or ham dinner for Easter, mimosas for a Mother's Day brunch of eggs Benedict, *tacos al pastor* for Cinco de Mayo, Memorial Day cookouts featuring sweet and smoky ribs, a buffet for a June graduation. When I became a New Yorker, new festivities and their food were added to the list. St. Patrick's Day (just a few days before the equinox, it signals the coming seasonal change, so I consider it more of a spring holiday than a winter one), with its raucous huge parade, was a day for everyone to party, Irish or not. I became slightly addicted to hamantaschen, the chunky, triangular cookies of Purim. I was invited to my first Passover seder and learned how to make a more-than-creditable beef brisket and other foods specific to that holy season. (Even when I can't stay for dinner, I deliver a beef brisket to one friend's house every year.)

In *Spring Gatherings*, I've collected my favorite recipes for this special time of renewal. Just as spring is the time for crocuses, tulips, and daffodils, it's also the time for green garlic, cherries, and rhubarb. I'll share recipes that use ingredients in season at the peak of their flavor. The next time you come across an unfamiliar item at the farmers' market, you're very likely to find a way to cook it here. Here are recipes, not just for special celebrations, but for anytime that you come together with friends and family. Whether it is a holiday feast on a table set with linen and crystal or a weeknight supper at the kitchen table, the meal will be much more satisfying when cooked with the season in mind.

Spring Gatherings

APPETIZERS

Fava Bean and Mint "Hummus"

Frittata with Asparagus, Prosciutto, and Chèvre

New Potatoes with Fresh Horseradish Dip with Garlic Chives

Shrimp and Avocado Cocktails with Chipotle Vinaigrette

Roasted Artichokes with Green Garlic Goddess Dip

Beer-Batter Okra with Curried Yogurt Dip

Mango-Ginger Mojitos

Berry Julepades

Fava Bean and Mint "Hummus"

This lovely hummus-like green puree looks and tastes like spring and is delicious spread on toasted pita or used as a dip for other vegetables. It's worth the effort it takes to shell and peel the fava beans.

1 large, plump head garlic

⅓ cup extra virgin olive oil, plus more for the garlic and for serving

Salt and freshly ground black pepper

2½ pounds fava beans

3 tablespoons fresh lemon juice

1 tablespoon chopped fresh mint, plus more for garnish

1. Position a rack in the center of the oven and preheat the oven to 400°F. Cut the garlic in half crosswise. Drizzle each cut surface with olive oil and season with salt and pepper to taste. Put the two halves back together, wrap in aluminum foil, and place on a baking sheet. Bake until the cloves are very tender and deep beige, about 40 minutes. Unwrap and set aside to cool. Squeeze the garlic out of the husks into a small bowl.

2. Meanwhile, remove the fava beans from their pods. Bring a large pot of lightly salted water to a boil over high heat. Add the fava beans and cook until the beans turn bright green, about 3 minutes. Drain and rinse under cold running water. Peel the fava beans.

3. Combine the peeled fava beans, roasted garlic, and lemon juice in a food processor fitted with the metal chopping blade. With the machine running, slowly add the ⅓ cup

olive oil, then 2 tablespoons water. Add the mint and pulse to combine. Season with salt and pepper to taste. (The spread can be prepared up to 3 days ahead, covered, and refrigerated.) Transfer to a small bowl, garnish with a drizzle of olive oil and some chopped mint, and serve.

Fava Beans

I'm warning you right now—preparing fava beans is a labor of love. The beans require a two-step process to ready them for eating. First, the beans are shucked from their fuzzy green pods and then they are blanched and peeled to remove their waxy skins. Your work will produce beautiful chartreuse beans with a buttery texture and a hint of bitterness to make their flavor interesting. Are they worth the trouble? I think so.

Enlist a friend or two to help with the prep work, for in the end, the big bunch of pods that you start with won't amount to a very large hill of beans. Expect to get about 1 cup of shelled beans for every pound of fava beans in the pods. And keep in mind that most people aren't familiar with fava beans, so reserve them for an appreciative audience. (Once, when I was unable to find fresh fava beans for a recipe, I substituted thawed frozen lima beans. I was lucky that no one noticed the difference.

I would not have been able to make the switch if I had been serving my Italian friends.)

Fava beans are one of the most popular foods in Mediterranean cooking, and every cuisine from the region has many recipes for the bean. Every spring, my Italian-born produce supplier provides daily commentary on when the first fava beans might arrive: "Next Tuesday, if it doesn't rain, or maybe Thursday . . ." He knows that when fava beans are very young, they only need to be shucked, and the cooked beans can be eaten skin and all, skipping that tedious final peeling. Do not serve uncooked fava beans, as they can be toxic to some people of Mediterranean extraction with a genetic allergy to them.

Frittata with Asparagus, Prosciutto, and Chèvre

Makes 4 to 6 servings

Without a doubt, frittata is one of the most versatile of dishes, suitable for brunch, supper, or lunch, and equally tasty served hot or at room temperature. This version features spring's asparagus, with accents of salty prosciutto and tangy goat cheese. Consider making it the main attraction at your Easter or Mother's Day brunch.

---

12 ounces asparagus spears, woody stems removed, cut into $\frac{1}{2}$-inch lengths

2 tablespoons olive oil, divided

2 ounces ($\frac{1}{4}$-inch dice) prosciutto

2 tablespoons finely chopped shallots

6 large eggs

$\frac{1}{2}$ teaspoon salt

$\frac{1}{8}$ teaspoon freshly ground black pepper

$\frac{1}{4}$ cup (1 ounce) crumbled rindless goat cheese (chèvre)

---

1. Bring a large pot of lightly salted water to a boil over high heat. Add the asparagus and cook until barely tender, 4 to 5 minutes. Drain in a colander, rinse under cold running water, and drain again. Pat dry with paper towels. Transfer to a plate.

2. Position a broiler rack 6 inches from the source of heat and preheat the broiler.

3. Heat 1 teaspoon of the oil in a nonstick medium skillet over medium-high heat. Add the prosciutto and cook, stirring occasionally, until it is lightly browned, about 3 minutes. Transfer to the plate with the asparagus.

4. Add 2 teaspoons oil to the skillet and heat. Add the shallots and cook, stirring often, until softened, about 2 minutes. Transfer to a medium bowl and set aside to cool slightly.

5. Add the eggs, salt, and pepper to the shallots. Whisk together until combined but not foamy. Add the asparagus and prosciutto. Add the remaining tablespoon of oil to the skillet and heat. Pour in the egg mixture and cook until the edges of the eggs begin to set, about 1 minute. Using a rubber spatula, lift up a section of the set portion of the eggs and tilt the skillet, letting the uncooked eggs run underneath. Continue to cook the eggs in this manner until the frittata is almost completely set, about 1 minute longer.

6. Transfer the skillet to the broiler (if the skillet handle isn't flameproof, wrap it in aluminum foil). Cook until the frittata is slightly puffed, about 1 minute.

7. Slide the frittata out of the skillet and onto a platter. Sprinkle the frittata with the cheese. Cut into wedges and serve hot or cool to room temperature.

New Potatoes with Fresh Horseradish Dip with Garlic Chives

Makes about 1¾ cups, or 8 to 12 servings

Garlic chives are one of the first herbs to show up in my garden, and pretty soon they're sporting pink flowers that are great for garnishing. Here they're combined with another boldly flavored spring stalwart, horseradish, as a dip for tiny new potatoes. Have fun with the potatoes by using whatever varieties the farmers' market has to offer. For an informal gathering, skip the new potatoes and just dunk potato chips or crisp fresh vegetables.

HORSERADISH-GARLIC CHIVE DIP

1 cup sour cream

½ cup mayonnaise

½ cup pared and shredded (use a micrograter) fresh horseradish

¼ cup minced fresh garlic chives or regular chives

Salt and freshly ground black pepper

Chive blossoms, for garnish (optional)

1½ pounds marble-sized red or white potatoes, scrubbed but not peeled

1. To make the dip, mix the sour cream, mayonnaise, horseradish, and chives together in a medium bowl. Season with salt and pepper to taste. Cover and refrigerate to blend the flavors for at least 2 hours or up to 2 days.

2. Place the potatoes in a large saucepan and add enough salted water to cover by 1 inch. Bring to a boil over high heat. Reduce the heat to medium-low and simmer until

the potatoes are tender when pierced with the tip of a sharp knife, about 15 minutes. Drain in a colander, rinse under cold running water, and drain again. Cool completely. Cut each potato in half.

3. Transfer the dip to a serving bowl and sprinkle with the chive blossoms, if using. Serve the potatoes with the dip.

Shrimp and Avocado Cocktails with Chipotle Vinaigrette

Makes 6 servings

Pretty in pink and pale green, these appetizers boast pastel spring hues. However, the zippy chipotle seasoning belies the subdued color. Remember, as with all avocado dishes, to think ahead and buy the avocados a few days in advance so they have plenty of time to ripen.

CHIPOTLE VINAIGRETTE

2 tablespoons fresh lime juice

2 tablespoons minced white or yellow onion

1 canned chipotle chile in adobo, minced

1 garlic clove, crushed through a press

$\frac{1}{2}$ cup extra virgin olive oil

Salt

1$\frac{1}{4}$ pounds large shrimp

3 avocados, pitted, peeled, and cut into $\frac{1}{2}$-inch dice

$\frac{1}{2}$ pint cherry or grape tomatoes, halved (1 cup)

1 tablespoon finely chopped cilantro, plus 6 cilantro sprigs

1. To make the vinaigrette, whisk the lime juice, onion, chipotle, and garlic together in a bowl. Gradually whisk in the oil. Season with salt to taste. (The vinaigrette can be prepared up to 1 day ahead, covered, and refrigerated. Whisk well before using.)

2. Bring a medium saucepan of lightly salted water to a boil over high heat. Add the shrimp and cook just until they turn opaque, about 3 minutes. Drain in a colander, rinse under cold running water, and drain again. Peel and devein 6 shrimp, leaving the tail segments attached, and set aside for garnish. Peel, devein, and coarsely chop the remaining shrimp. Cover and refrigerate the whole and chopped shrimp until well chilled, at least 2 hours. (The shrimp can be prepared up to 8 hours ahead.)

3. Gently toss the avocados with 2 tablespoons of the chipotle dressing. Add the chopped shrimp, cherry tomatoes, and chopped cilantro and toss again. Season with salt to taste. Divide evenly among six glasses. Drizzle with the remaining vinaigrette. (The cocktails can be covered and chilled for up to 1 hour before serving.)

4. Top each cocktail with a whole shrimp and a cilantro sprig and serve chilled.

Roasted Artichokes with Green Garlic Goddess Dip

Just like most cooks, the only way I knew how to cook artichokes was by boiling them in a big pot of water. Not a bad method, but when I figured out how to roast them (actually a hybrid steaming-roasting process), there was no turning back. Boiling obviously dilutes the flavor of the artichokes, while roasting intensifies their taste. Green goddess dressing, which originated in San Francisco, is one of my favorite dips, and a perfect match for the meaty artichoke flesh. But when it is made with spring's green garlic, it is truly a dip for the gods.

GREEN GARLIC GODDESS DIP

1½ teaspoons anchovy paste

2 tablespoons fresh lemon juice

1 cup mayonnaise

½ cup sour cream

1 green garlic stalk or scallion, white and green parts, minced

2 tablespoons minced fresh parsley

1 tablespoon minced fresh tarragon

Freshly ground black pepper

6 artichokes

1 lemon, cut in half

2 tablespoons olive oil

Salt and freshly ground black pepper

1. To make the dip, dissolve the anchovy paste in the lemon juice in a medium bowl. Add the mayonnaise, sour cream, garlic stalk, parsley, and tarragon and mix until combined. Season with pepper to taste. Cover and refrigerate to blend the flavors, at least 1 hour and up to 2 days.

2. Position a rack in the center of the oven and preheat the oven to 400°F. One at a time, cut the top inch from each artichoke. If the artichoke stem is attached, cut it off. Then rub the top and bottom of the artichoke with a lemon half and stand it in a flameproof roasting pan just large enough to hold the 6 artichokes without crowding. If desired, pare the thick green skin from each artichoke stem and add the stems to the pan. Squeeze the juice from the lemon halves over the artichokes, drizzle with the oil, and season with salt and pepper to taste. Pour in enough water to come ¼ inch up the sides of the pan. Bring to a boil on the stove over high heat. Cover tightly with a double thickness of aluminum foil (or the pan's lid, if it has one).

3. Roast until one of the bottom leaves pulls easily from an artichoke, 45 to 60 minutes, depending on the size of the artichokes. Remove the artichokes from the pan and drain upside down on a large platter. (Transfer the stems to the platter, if using.) Let cool until warm or cool completely.

4. Transfer the dip to individual ramekins. Serve the artichokes with the dip and bowls to hold the scraped artichoke leaves.

Beer-Batter Okra with Curried Yogurt Dip

Makes 6 to 8 servings

As I'm writing this, I realize that there are a lot of dips in this chapter! I shouldn't be surprised, as whenever I want a surefire appetizer, my thoughts turn to dips—everyone loves them. The same cannot be said for okra. However, when I batter and deep-fry the okra until golden and serve it with this mildly spicy yogurt dip, I rarely have a single piece left on the platter.

CURRIED YOGURT DIP

1 teaspoon vegetable oil

2 scallions, white and green parts separated and finely chopped

2 teaspoons Madras-style curry powder

1 cup plain low-fat yogurt

BEER BATTER

¾ cup lager beer

1 large egg

1 cup flour

1 teaspoon baking soda

1 teaspoon salt

¼ teaspoon freshly ground black pepper

Vegetable oil, for deep-frying

1 pound okra, stems trimmed

Salt, for serving

1. To make the dip, heat the oil in a medium skillet over medium heat. Add the scallion whites and cook, stirring occasionally, until tender, about 3 minutes. Add the curry powder and stir until fragrant, about 15 seconds. Scrape into a medium bowl. Let cool. Add the yogurt and scallion greens and stir together. Cover and refrigerate to blend the flavors, at least 1 hour and up to 1 day.

2. To make the batter, whisk the beer and egg together in a medium bowl. Add the flour, baking soda, salt, and pepper and whisk just until smooth. Cover and let stand at room temperature for 30 minutes.

3. Pour enough oil to come about 2 inches up the sides of a large, heavy saucepan and heat over high heat until a deep-frying thermometer reads 350°F. Line a baking sheet with wire cake racks.

4. Working in two or three batches, add the okra to the batter to coat. Lift the okra from the batter, letting the excess batter drip back into the bowl, and carefully add the okra to the oil, taking care not to add too many pieces to the oil, lest they stick together or the oil boils over. Deep-fry until golden brown, about 2 minutes. Using a wire skimmer or a slotted spoon, transfer the okra to the wire racks to drain. Season with the salt and serve hot with the dip.

Mango-Ginger Mojitos

Makes 4 drinks

Mojitos are usually made from ingredients crushed together in the serving glass. But, for practicality's sake, the method is streamlined in this version. These were the hit of a Memorial Day barbecue one year, and now they're standard fare at all of our neighborhood cookouts. I also recommend them to replace the standard mimosas at a Sunday brunch.

½ cup sugar

8 quarter-sized slices peeled fresh ginger

1 cup packed mint leaves, plus 4 sprigs for garnish

1 ripe mango, pitted, peeled, and coarsely chopped

¾ cup silver rum

½ cup fresh lime juice

1 cup chilled club soda, as needed, for serving

4 lime rounds, for garnish

1. Bring the sugar, ginger, and ½ cup water to a boil in a medium saucepan over medium heat, stirring to dissolve the sugar. Remove from the heat and add the mint. Cover and let stand for 10 minutes. Strain in a wire sieve over a bowl, pressing hard on the solids to extract the flavors. Discard the solids.

2. Puree the mango, ginger-mint syrup, rum, and lime juice in a blender. Transfer to a pitcher. (The mango mixture can be prepared up to 8 hours ahead.)

3. When ready to serve, fill four tall glasses with ice. Divide the mango mixture among the glasses and top off each with club soda. Add a swizzle stick to each mojito so the guests can stir them. Garnish each glass with a lime round and a mint sprig, and serve at once.

Berry Julepades

Every May, countless mint juleps are served at Kentucky Derby parties, but not everyone loves their bourbon in such undiluted proportions. Here's a mint-and-bourbon-based punch with plenty of fruit flavors to help it go down smoothly. It's just as drinkable with vodka substituted for the bourbon.

1 cup sugar

1 cup packed mint leaves, plus 8 sprigs for garnish

1 pound strawberries, hulled and sliced

1 cup fresh lemon juice

1 cup bourbon

1. Bring the sugar, mint leaves, and 1 cup water to a boil in a medium saucepan over high heat, stirring often to dissolve the sugar. Remove from the heat and let stand for 30 minutes. Strain in a sieve over a bowl, pressing hard on the solids. Discard the solids.

2. Puree the strawberries and mint syrup together in a blender. Transfer to a large pitcher. Add the lemon juice, bourbon, and 3 cups water and stir well. Cover and refrigerate until chilled, at least 3 hours.

3. Serve in tall glasses over ice, garnished with a mint sprig.

SOUPS AND SALADS

Vidalia Onion Soup with Cheddar Toasts

Chilled Pea Vichyssoise

Asparagus and Spinach Soup with Mascarpone

Roasted Asparagus with Caesar Dressing

Sugar Snap Peas with Chive Vinaigrette

Watercress Salad with Mangoes and Almonds

Couscous Salad with Radishes and Peas

Strawberry, Hazelnut, and Chèvre Salad with Strawberry Vinaigrette

Vidalia Onion Soup with Cheddar Toasts

Makes 6 servings

A direct descendant of French onion soup, this version with translucent tangles of Vidalia onions and a gooey topping of melted sharp Cheddar cheese is really too filling to serve as a first course. Instead, pair it with a green salad and a glass of red wine for a light supper on a cool spring night. I also recommend using homemade beef stock as a base, since I have yet to find a canned version I like enough to eat by the bowlful!

3 tablespoons unsalted butter

3 pounds Vidalia or other sweet onions, cut into thin half-moons

1 cup hearty red wine, such as Shiraz-Cabernet blend

8 cups homemade beef stock or canned low-sodium beef broth

1½ tablespoons red wine vinegar

2 teaspoons chopped fresh thyme or 1 teaspoon dried thyme

1 bay leaf

Salt and freshly ground black pepper

12 baguette slices, toasted

1 cup (4 ounces) shredded sharp Cheddar

1. Melt the butter in a heavy-bottomed soup pot over medium heat. Stir in the onions and cover. Cook, stirring occasionally, until they begin to soften, about 5 minutes. Reduce the heat to medium-low. Cover again and cook, stirring occasionally, until the onions are deep golden brown and very tender, about 25 minutes.

2. Stir in the wine. Increase the heat to high and bring to a boil. Cook until the wine is reduced by half, about 3 minutes. Stir in the stock, vinegar, thyme, and bay leaf and bring to a boil. Reduce the heat to medium-low and simmer until full-flavored, about 30 minutes. Season with salt and pepper to taste. Remove the bay leaf.

3. Position a broiler rack about 6 inches from the source of heat and preheat the broiler.

4. Ladle the soup into six large flameproof soup crocks. Place two toasts in each crock and sprinkle with the Cheddar. Broil until the cheese is melted and bubbling, about 1 minute. Serve immediately.

Vidalia Onions

Bite into a sweet onion and you won't mistake it for a piece of cake. Thanks to a reduced amount of the sulfuric compounds that irritate your eyes when it is cut, a sweet onion simply isn't as sharp as a regular yellow onion. Also, a sweet onion has more water, which dilutes the irritants. Even if it's not candy-sweet, its lack of pungency makes it popular with many cooks.

Sweet onions are grown all over the United States. Walla Wallas from Washington, Texas 1015s from the Lone Star State, and Mauis from Hawaii are just three of the large group that keeps the market supplied year-round. But Vidalias, produced in a twenty-county area in southeastern Georgia, are strictly a spring crop. Hand-harvested from April to June, these distinctive, flat-top onions are more expensive than their counterparts. To enjoy Vidalia onions past their harvest, individually wrap them in newspaper and store them in a cool, dark place away from potatoes, which can give off moisture and make the onions soft.

While sweet onions won't bring you to tears, they should not be substituted for yellow onions in your everyday cooking. There are times when the bitterness of a yellow onion is needed to balance other ingredients, such as carrots and tomatoes. Vidalias are best served raw in salads or cooked until caramelized and deliciously tender.

Chilled Pea Vichyssoise

Makes 6 servings

Vichyssoise, the renowned chilled leek and potato soup, can be on the bland side, both in flavor and looks. However, with the addition of peas to the basic recipe, the result is gorgeous to look at and delicious to eat. If you would like a garnish, drizzle a little heavy cream over each serving.

2 pounds peas in the pod

4 cups canned low-sodium chicken broth

1 tablespoon vegetable oil

2 medium leeks, white and pale green parts only, chopped (1½ cups)

1 medium russet potato (7 ounces), peeled and cut into ½-inch cubes

Salt and freshly ground black pepper

1. Shell the peas, reserving half the pods. You should have 2 cups shelled peas. Coarsely chop the reserved pods. Combine the chopped pods and broth in a large saucepan and bring to a boil over high heat. Reduce the heat to medium-low and simmer for 10 minutes. Strain over a bowl, pressing hard on the pods, and set the broth aside. Discard the pods.

2. Heat the oil in a soup pot over medium heat. Add the leeks and cover. Cook, stirring occasionally, until softened, about 3 minutes. Add the potato, peas, and broth and cover. Increase the heat to high and bring to a boil. Return the heat to medium-low and set the lid ajar. Simmer until the potatoes are tender, about 20 minutes.

3. In batches, puree in a blender, being sure that the blender lid is ajar. Pour into a bowl. Season with salt and pepper to taste. Let cool until tepid, about 2 hours. Cover and refrigerate until chilled, at least 4 hours.

4. Season again (chilled foods dull the taste of the seasonings) and serve chilled.

Asparagus and Spinach Soup with Mascarpone

Makes 6 to 8 servings

This lovely soup, bursting with vegetable flavor, is a fine choice as an opener to a special meal, although it can also be served as a light lunch. The slightly tart mascarpone adds a bit of acidity, which balances the mellow soup—while an enrichment of heavy cream may seem as if it will do the same thing, it doesn't have the necessary sharpness that perks up the flavor.

2 tablespoons unsalted butter

¼ cup chopped shallots

2 pounds asparagus, woody stems removed, cut into 1-inch lengths

8 ounces fresh spinach leaves, well rinsed, stemmed, and coarsely chopped

⅓ cup uncooked long-grain rice

4 cups canned low-sodium chicken broth

1 tablespoon fresh lemon juice

Salt and freshly ground black pepper

½ cup mascarpone, or as needed, at room temperature

1. Melt the butter in a large saucepan over medium heat. Add the shallots and cook, stirring occasionally, until softened, about 3 minutes.

2. Add the asparagus, spinach, and rice and stir well. Add the broth and bring to a boil over high heat. Reduce the heat to medium-low and cover. Simmer until the asparagus and rice are very tender, about 20 minutes. Remove from the heat and stir in the lemon juice.

3. In batches, puree in a blender, making sure that the lid is ajar. Transfer to a soup tureen and season with salt and pepper to taste.

4. Ladle into bowls and top each serving with a dollop of mascarpone. Serve hot.

Roasted Asparagus with Caesar Dressing

One Mother's Day, I needed something to round out a buffet and I created this dish. Now it makes an appearance at almost all of my springtime parties. Nothing brings out the flavor of asparagus like roasting. If you prefer, boil the asparagus instead, but grilling adds a smoky note that may be too intense for the dressing.

DRESSING

¾ cup mayonnaise

2 tablespoons fresh lemon juice

2 garlic cloves, minced or crushed through a press

½ teaspoon anchovy paste

¼ teaspoon freshly ground black pepper

ROASTED ASPARAGUS

Olive oil, for the baking sheet

2 pounds asparagus, woody ends discarded

¼ cup freshly grated Romano or Parmesan

1. To make the dressing, whisk the mayonnaise, lemon juice, garlic, anchovy paste, and pepper in a medium bowl until combined. Cover and refrigerate for at least 1 hour and up to 3 days to blend the flavors.

2. Position a rack in the top part of the oven and preheat the oven to 450°F. Lightly oil a large rimmed baking sheet.

3. Spread the asparagus on the baking sheet in a single layer. Roast until the asparagus is bright green and barely tender, 10 to 15 minutes, depending on the thickness of the spears. Cool to room temperature.

4. Arrange the asparagus on a platter, with the spears facing the same direction. Spoon the dressing over the asparagus and sprinkle with the cheese. Serve at room temperature.

Sugar Snap Peas with Chive Vinaigrette

Makes 6 servings

This modest recipe proves that when you have excellent, full-flavored produce in season, you don't need to do much to it to create a memorable dish. The lemon-chive vinaigrette is the lightest dressing for the sugar snaps, but the flavors are in perfect understated harmony. Once it's dressed, don't let the salad stand much longer than thirty minutes or the dressing could discolor the sugar snaps. If you have chive blossoms, add a sprinkle as a finishing garnish. The purple flowers are a great complementary color to the green sugar snap peas.

12 ounces sugar snap peas, trimmed

1 tablespoon fresh lemon juice

¼ teaspoon salt

A few grinds of black pepper

¼ cup extra virgin olive oil

2 tablespoons finely chopped fresh chives

Grated zest of 1 lemon

Fresh chive blossoms, for garnish (optional)

1. Bring a medium saucepan of lightly salted water to a boil over high heat. Add the sugar snap peas and cook just until crisp-tender, about 3 minutes. Drain in a colander, rinse under cold running water, and drain again. Pat dry with paper towels.

2. Combine the lemon juice, salt, and pepper in a medium bowl and gradually whisk in the oil. Stir in the chives. Add the sugar snap peas and stir gently.

3. Transfer to a serving bowl. Sprinkle with the lemon zest and the chive blossoms, if using. Serve immediately.

Derby Day Buffet

Beer-Batter Okra with Curried Yogurt Dip (page 17)

Berry Julepades (page 22)

Barbecued Beef Ribs with Cherry-Chipotle Sauce (page 53)

Sugar Snap Peas with Chive Vinaigrette (page 37)

Couscous Salad with Radishes and Peas (page 42)

Kentucky Derby Ice Cream Sundaes with Bourbon Pecan Sauce (page 162)

Watercress Salad with Mangoes and Almonds

When I am stumped for a first course, I often turn to this salad, which is sure to pique the appetites of my dinner guests. The combination of bright green and orange is attractive to look at, while the flavors of the sweet mangoes and peppery watercress play off the crunchy, salty almonds.

2 tablespoons sherry vinegar

¼ teaspoon salt

⅛ teaspoon freshly ground black pepper

½ cup olive oil

12 ounces watercress, tough stems removed

2 ripe mangoes, pitted, peeled, and thinly sliced

½ cup Marcona almonds (see Note)

1. Whisk the vinegar, salt, and pepper together in a large bowl. Gradually whisk in the oil.

2. Add the watercress and mango and toss gently. Transfer to dinner plates. Scatter an equal amount of the almonds over each salad and serve immediately.

Note: *Roasted in oil and tossed with sea salt, Marcona almonds are imported from Spain. You'll find them at specialty food stores. If you wish, substitute ¼ cup sliced natural almonds, toasted in a 350°F oven until lightly browned, about 8 minutes.*

Couscous Salad with Radishes and Peas

Makes 4 to 6 servings

This attractive salad sports spring colors of pink, green, and yellow, but it's not just another pretty face. Versatile as they come, it works equally well on a buffet as it does as a side salad for grilled salmon. This salad is best served at room temperature, not chilled.

Salt

1 pound peas in the pod, shelled (1 cup shelled peas)

1½ cups (10 ounces) quick-cooking couscous

2 tablespoons fresh lemon juice

Freshly ground black pepper

½ cup extra virgin olive oil

1 cup thinly sliced radishes

2 scallions, white and green parts, finely chopped

2 tablespoons chopped fresh mint

1. Bring a saucepan of lightly salted water to a boil over high heat. Add the peas and cook until tender, about 7 minutes. Drain in a wire sieve, rinse under cold running water, and drain again. Pat dry with paper towels. Set aside.

2. Bring 2 cups water and ½ teaspoon salt to a boil in a medium saucepan over high heat. Stir in the couscous. Remove from the heat and cover tightly. Let stand until the couscous is tender, about 5 minutes.

3. Whisk the lemon juice, $1/4$ teaspoon salt, and $1/8$ teaspoon freshly ground black pepper together in a medium bowl. Gradually whisk in the oil. Add the couscous and mix, fluffing the couscous with a fork. Let cool.

4. Stir in the reserved peas with the radishes, scallions, and mint. Season with salt and pepper to taste. Serve at room temperature.

Radishes

I was never a big fan of radishes. In my family, they were what you put in salads when you were out of tomatoes. They added a little color and lots of peppery flavor, but my young palate didn't appreciate their forthright heat.

Then one day in the south of France, I was served a radish sandwich, with thin slices of the freshest radishes on a slice of crusty bread slathered with sweet butter and a sprinkle of sea salt. The precise variety was French Breakfast, a gorgeous, hot-pink, elongated radish with a splash of white at the tip. Maybe I liked it because, among the many radish varieties, it is one of the mildest. Like all radishes, it had a pleasing crispness that any other vegetable would kill for.

Radishes are members of the mustard family (*Brassicaceae*), which accounts for their spiciness. They grow very quickly and can go from seed to harvest in just a few weeks. Try them as part of your crudité platter, served with a cool creamy dip to offset the radishes' heat. They are also surprisingly delicious when thinly sliced and sautéed in butter until crisp-tender. In other words, they are quite versatile and can hold their own outside of the salad bowl.

Strawberry, Hazelnut, and Chèvre Salad with Strawberry Vinaigrette

Makes 6 servings

At first glance, this combination may seem more appropriate for dessert than for a first course. But, encouraged by seeing such recipes on many restaurant menus, I decided to make my own version and it was a winner, perfect for spring entertaining. The interplay of the sweet berries, tart cheese, crisp nuts, and fresh greens is refreshing, and a real appetite rouser.

⅓ cup hazelnuts

1 pound strawberries, hulled

⅓ cup hazelnut oil (see Note)

2 tablespoons balsamic vinegar

Salt and freshly ground black pepper

8 ounces mixed baby greens (mesclun)

4 ounces rindless goat cheese (chèvre), crumbled

1. Position a rack in the center of the oven and preheat the oven to 350°F. Spread the hazelnuts on a baking sheet. Bake, stirring occasionally, until the skins are split and the nuts underneath are toasted, about 10 minutes. Transfer to a clean kitchen towel. Wrap the nuts in the towel and let stand 10 minutes. Rub the nuts in the towel to remove as much of the skins as possible. Coarsely chop the nuts.

2. Puree 5 of the largest strawberries in a blender; you should have ¼ cup strawberry puree. Add the oil and vinegar and process until thickened. Season with salt and pepper to taste.

3. Slice the remaining strawberries. Toss the sliced strawberries, mesclun, hazelnuts, and strawberry vinaigrette together in a large bowl. Transfer to plates, sprinkle with the crumbled goat cheese, and serve immediately.

Note: *Hazelnut oil is pricey, but I use it (and walnut oil, too) often in my cooking. As it tends to go rancid fairly quickly, store the oil in the refrigerator, where it will keep for about six months, and bring to room temperature before using. If you wish, you can make a good substitute. Process $1/4$ cup toasted skinned hazelnuts and $1/3$ cup vegetable oil in a blender. Let stand 10 minutes, then strain through a fine wire sieve.*

Strawberries

Even though the supermarket variety is available year-round, if you want true strawberry flavor, wait for the berries' annual springtime appearance.

There are actually three main types of strawberries, each named for the length of sunlight exposure needed to spur flower growth: short day, long day, and day neutral (this last variety produces flowers regardless of sunlight exposure). June-bearing cultivars give just one harvest in late spring (I usually serve a strawberry-rhubarb dessert at my Memorial Day barbecue); ever-bearing berries will bear repeatedly throughout the summer.

Strawberries, like all berries, are pretty perishable. Recently, a study by food scientist Harold McGee showed that submerging the berries in very hot (125°F) water for 30 seconds lengthened the time before molding by a few days. You'll need an instant-read thermometer and a timer, because precision counts here, but it works. Dry the berries well on paper towels before storing in the refrigerator.

MAIN COURSES

Ale-Braised Corned Beef with Vegetables

Oven-Braised Beef Brisket with Green Herb Sauce

Barbecued Beef Ribs with Cherry-Chipotle Sauce

Tacos al Pastor with Pineapple-Radish Salsa

Marinated Grilled Pork Chops with Apricots

Roast Rack of Lamb with Mint Béarnaise

Chicken Breast and Baby Artichoke Fricassee

Duck Breasts with Rhubarb-Cherry Chutney

Halibut with Sorrel Sauce

Salmon with Fresh Horseradish Crust

Asparagus, Ham, and Poached Eggs on Cheese Polenta

Ale-Braised Corned Beef with Vegetables

Makes 8 servings

Although Saint Patrick's Day officially occurs during winter, I consider it the first spring holiday, since it is only three days away from the equinox. Of course, corned beef for dinner is a must (along with the Irish Soda Bread on page 124)! Simmering the brisket in ale with lots of spices helps cut through the meat's saltiness. Be forewarned that corned beef shrinks like crazy, and it is a good idea to simmer two briskets for sufficient servings—and to supply leftovers for sandwiches and corned beef hash. Also, rather than crowding the vegetables into the pot with the beef, this recipe solves the problem by cooking the meat first.

CORNED BEEF

Two 3-pound corned beef briskets

Two 12-ounce bottles pale ale

1 teaspoon coriander seed

1 teaspoon black peppercorns

1 teaspoon yellow mustard seed

½ teaspoon whole allspice

¼ teaspoon whole cloves

2 bay leaves

8 medium red-skinned potatoes, scrubbed but unpeeled

8 carrots, or 4 carrots and 4 parsnips, cut into 1-inch lengths

One 2¼-pound green cabbage, cut lengthwise into 8 wedges

5 tablespoons unsalted butter, well softened

2 tablespoons chopped fresh parsley

Prepared mustard, for serving

1. Layer the beef in a very large Dutch oven or a metal roasting pan with a lid. Pour in the ale and add enough water to barely cover the beef. Rinse a 12-inch square piece of cheesecloth and wring it dry. Wrap the coriander, peppercorns, mustard seed, allspice, cloves, and bay leaves in the cheesecloth, and tie into a bundle (or place the spices in a tea ball). Add to the Dutch oven. Cover and bring to a boil over high heat.

2. Reduce the heat to medium-low. Simmer, adding hot water to the Dutch oven occasionally if needed to keep the beef submerged, until the beef is fork-tender, $2\frac{1}{2}$ to 3 hours.

3. Meanwhile, preheat the oven to its lowest setting, about 175°F. When the corned beef is tender, transfer it to a shallow roasting pan. Add 1 cup cooking liquid to the pan and cover with aluminum foil. Keep warm in the oven while cooking the vegetables.

4. Remove the spice bag from the Dutch oven and discard. Add the potatoes to the cooking liquid in the Dutch oven and increase the heat to medium to bring the liquid to a moderate boil. Cook, uncovered, for 15 minutes. Add the carrots and cabbage. Cook until the potatoes are tender, about 15 minutes longer.

5. Mash the butter and parsley together in a small bowl. Using a slotted spoon, transfer the vegetables to a large bowl, adding dollops of the parsley butter.

6. Transfer the corned beef to a carving board, and cut across the grain into thin slices. Arrange the slices on a platter. Serve hot, with the vegetables and the mustard passed on the side.

Oven-Braised Beef Brisket with Green Herb Sauce

Makes 8 to 10 servings

Brisket often stars as the main course at the Passover seder, but most versions are on the heavy side and served with hearty sauces, which are really more appropriate for winter dining. This version is much lighter and is served with a bright green herb sauce that sings of spring. Do try to cook the brisket the day before serving, as resting the meat makes it much easier to slice. And while you can certainly cook only one brisket, I find that, for the time involved, it makes sense to cook two at once.

BRISKET

Two 3-pound first-cut beef briskets

1 tablespoon kosher salt

1 teaspoon dried thyme

¾ teaspoon freshly ground black pepper

2 tablespoons olive oil

2 medium onions, sliced

6 garlic cloves, minced

2 bay leaves

GREEN SAUCE

1 garlic clove, peeled

2 cups packed chopped fresh parsley

4 scallions, white and green parts, trimmed and coarsely chopped

3 tablespoons freshly grated or drained prepared horseradish, or more to taste

1½ tablespoons Dijon mustard

Grated zest of 1 lemon

2 tablespoons fresh lemon juice

½ cup extra virgin olive oil

Salt and freshly ground black pepper

1. The day before serving, make the brisket. Position a rack in the lower third of the oven and preheat the oven to 300°F. Rinse the briskets and pat dry with paper towels. Mix the salt, thyme, and pepper. Rub the salt mixture all over the briskets.

2. Heat the oil in a large Dutch oven over medium-high heat. Add 1 brisket to the pot and brown on both sides, about 5 minutes. Transfer to a platter. Repeat with the remaining brisket. Add the onions, garlic, and bay leaves, stir well, but do not cook. Return the browned briskets to the pot (they can overlap, as they will shrink during cooking). Add enough water to barely cover the briskets. Bring to a boil over high heat. Cover tightly.

3. Bake, turning the briskets over after 1¼ hours, until the meat is fork-tender, about 2½ hours. Remove from the oven and uncover. Let the briskets stand in the cooking liquid in a cool place (but not the refrigerator) until tepid, about 1 hour. Cover and refrigerate overnight.

4. Meanwhile, make the green sauce. Fit a food processor with the metal chopping blade. With the machine running, drop the garlic through the feed tube to mince it. Add the parsley, scallions, horseradish, mustard, and lemon zest and juice. Process until finely chopped. With the machine running, add the oil in a slow stream through

the feed tube and process, scraping down the sides of the bowl as needed, until smooth. Season with salt and pepper to taste. Transfer to a bowl and cover tightly. (The sauce can be made up to 1 day ahead. Stir well before using.)

5. The next day, scrape off as much hardened fat from the surface of the cooking liquid as possible. Remove the briskets from the cooking liquid and transfer the meat to a carving board. Cut across the grain into ¼-inch-thick slices. Do not cut the briskets too thinly or they will fall apart during reheating. Bring the cooking liquid to a simmer over medium heat. Return the sliced briskets to the pot and cook just until heated through, about 5 minutes.

6. Using a slotted spatula, transfer the sliced briskets to a serving platter. Spoon about ¼ cup of the hot cooking liquid over the meat. (Strain the remaining cooking liquid and use it in recipes that call for beef stock.). Serve hot, with the green sauce passed on the side.

Barbecued Beef Ribs with Cherry-Chipotle Sauce

Makes 6 servings

Barbecue season officially begins on Memorial Day, if not before. As soon as cherries show up at my market in late May, I cook up a big batch of this fruity-spicy sauce to slather onto my grilled meats and poultry. Of course, it is great with pork baby back or spareribs, but it is also fantastic on their kissin' cousins, meaty and chewy beef ribs. The trick to these ribs is to cook them low and slow at an average temperature of 300°F. (It can fluctuate 25°F in either direction, so don't get too obsessive!) Most gas grills come equipped with a thermometer in their lids to help tell the temperature, but charcoal grills do not. To gauge the temperature on a charcoal grill, drop a metal-stemmed deep-frying thermometer through one of the vent holes in the lid and add more briquets when the temperature drops below 275°F.

CHERRY-CHIPOTLE BARBECUE SAUCE

1 tablespoon vegetable oil

⅓ cup chopped shallots

1 garlic clove, minced

2 cups (about 14 ounces) pitted cherries

1 cup tomato ketchup

½ cup cider vinegar

½ cup packed light brown sugar

1 or 2 canned chipotle chiles in adobo, minced

Beef Ribs

5 pounds beef ribs, for barbecuing (see Note)

1 tablespoon kosher salt

1 teaspoon freshly ground black pepper

Two 12-ounce cans lager beer

1. To make the sauce, heat the oil in a saucepan over medium heat. Add the shallots and cook, stirring occasionally, until lightly browned, about 3 minutes. Stir in the garlic and cook until fragrant, about 30 seconds. Add the cherries, ketchup, vinegar, and brown sugar and bring to a simmer. Reduce the heat to medium-low and simmer, stirring often, until the cherries are very tender, about 15 minutes. Stir in the chipotle chiles to taste. Transfer to a blender and puree. Cool completely. Makes about 3 cups.

2. Build a charcoal fire with about 3 pounds of briquets on one side of an outdoor grill. Let the fire burn down for about 30 minutes, or until you can hold your hand over the coals at the grill grate level for about 4 seconds. If using a gas grill, preheat one side on high and leave the other side off. Cover the grill and adjust the heat until the grill thermometer reads 300°F. In either case, place an empty 13 x 9-inch disposable aluminum foil pan on the empty side of the grill.

3. Slip the tip of a dinner knife under the thin membrane on the bony side of the rib slab. Using a paper towel, grab one end of the membrane and pull it off the slab. Cut the slabs into 4 or 5 manageable portions. Season with the salt and pepper.

4. Place a metal rib rack or V-shaped roasting rack in the aluminum pan. Stand the ribs on the rack. Add 1 cup water to the foil pan. Cover and grill, drizzling about ½ cup of the beer over the ribs every 45 minutes or so (and adding about 12 briquets to the

charcoal fire to maintain an average temperature of 300°F), until the meat is tender when pierced with the tip of a knife, about 3 hours. Transfer the ribs to a large baking sheet. Remove the foil pan.

5. Add more briquets to the grill and let burn until covered with white ash. Spread the coals out in an even layer. For a gas grill, increase the heat to high.

6. Place the ribs on the grill and cover. Grill, turning occasionally, until sizzling, about 4 minutes. Brush with the sauce and continue grilling until glazed, about 4 minutes more. Transfer to a carving board and let stand for a few minutes.

7. Cut into individual ribs. Transfer the ribs to a serving platter. Serve hot, with any remaining sauce passed on the side.

Note: *Beef ribs for barbecue are cut from the rib section. Do not confuse them with short ribs or flanken (cross-cut short ribs). If you get them at a wholesale club, as I do, the ribs will come in large slabs and the membrane should be removed. Supermarket beef ribs are usually cut into individual ribs, so removing the membrane is tedious and not worth the trouble. These ribs will just be a little more chewy at the bone.*

Tacos al Pastor with Pineapple-Radish Salsa

Tacos al pastor ("shepherd's style" tacos in Spanish) are stuffed with grilled, chile-marinated pork and juicy pineapple. During one spring visit I took to Mexico, the pineapple was supplemented with radishes, which added their own crunch and zip to the proceedings. My version is much easier than the classic, but it doesn't make it any less delicious.

PORK AND MARINADE

¾ cup canned or fresh pineapple juice (see Note)

1 tablespoon pure ground ancho chile or chili powder

½ teaspoon dried oregano

Pinch of ground cinnamon

Pinch of ground cloves

½ teaspoon kosher salt

2 pork tenderloins (about 2¼ pounds), silver skin trimmed

PINEAPPLE-RADISH SALSA

1 ripe pineapple, peeled, cored, and cut lengthwise into quarters

½ cup thinly sliced radishes

¼ cup chopped red onion

2 tablespoons finely chopped fresh cilantro

Pinch of salt

24 corn tortillas

1. To make the marinade, whisk the pineapple juice, ground chile, oregano, cinnamon, cloves, and salt together in a nonreactive bowl. Pour into a zippered plastic bag. Add the pork. Refrigerate, turning the bag occasionally, for at least 1 and up to 8 hours. Remove from the refrigerator 30 minutes before grilling. Drain the pork, but do not scrape off the chile clinging to the surface.

2. Meanwhile, make the salsa. Cut one pineapple quarter into $1/2$-inch dice (you should have 2 cups). Reserve the remaining pineapple for another use. Combine the pineapple, radishes, onion, cilantro, and salt. Set aside at room temperature for at least 30 minutes and up to 2 hours.

3. Build a charcoal fire in an outdoor grill. Bank the coals so one side is higher than the other. If using a gas grill, preheat the grill, then turn one half of the cooking area to high and the other half to low.

4. Lightly oil the grill grate. Place the tenderloins on the hotter area of the grill and cover. Grill, turning occasionally, until the tenderloins are seared with grill marks, about 5 minutes. Move the pork to the cooler area of the grill and continue grilling, turning occasionally, until an instant-read thermometer inserted in the thickest part of the pork reads 145°F, 10 to 12 minutes. Transfer to a carving board and let stand for 5 minutes.

5. Meanwhile, in batches, place the tortillas on the grill and cook, turning once, until heated through. Transfer to a napkin-lined bowl or basket and wrap in the napkin to keep warm.

6. Using a sharp, thin knife, cut the pork crosswise into ¼-inch-thick rounds. Transfer to a bowl and add any carving juices. To serve, allow each guest to stack two tortillas (the pork and salsa are quite juicy and may leak through a single tortilla) and add the sliced pork and salsa.

Note: *Since you need only a quarter of a pineapple for the salsa, you will have leftover pineapple that can be juiced for the marinade. You don't need an expensive expeller juicer. Simply peel, core, and coarsely chop enough pineapple to make 4 cups. Process the pineapple in a food processor or blender until coarsely ground. Strain in a wire sieve over a bowl, pressing hard on the pineapple with a rubber spatula to extract the juices. Measure out ¾ cup fresh pineapple juice for the marinade. If you don't have enough, add water and a splash of cider vinegar to make up the difference.*

Marinated Grilled Pork Chops with Apricots

Makes 4 servings

Most cooks are familiar with marinating and grilling meat, but there are also fruits that can be prepared this way, either as an accompaniment to the main course or as a separate dessert. In the former category, the combination of pork and apricots is highly complementary, especially when served with a soy-bourbon sauce made from the marinade. This dish has become a favorite at my late spring cookouts, served with steamed rice to soak up the sauce.

MARINADE

½ cup soy sauce

½ cup bourbon

3 tablespoons light brown sugar

3 tablespoons peeled and minced fresh ginger

1 tablespoon dark Asian sesame oil

3 garlic cloves, minced

¼ teaspoon five-spice powder

¼ teaspoon freshly ground black pepper

Four (1-inch thick) center-cut pork loin chops

6 ripe apricots, halved and pitted

2 teaspoons vegetable oil

1 teaspoon cornstarch, dissolved in 1 tablespoon cold water

1. To make the marinade, whisk the soy sauce, bourbon, brown sugar, ginger, sesame oil, garlic, five-spice powder, and pepper together in a medium bowl to dissolve the sugar. Pour half the marinade into a zippered plastic bag, reserving the remaining marinade. Add the pork to the bag. Refrigerate for at least 1 and up to 8 hours. Remove from the refrigerator 1 hour before grilling.

2. Build a charcoal fire in an outdoor grill. Bank the coals so one side is higher than the other. If using a gas grill, preheat the grill, then turn half of the cooking area to high and the other half to low.

3. Lightly oil the grill grate. Remove the pork from the marinade, discarding the marinade in the bag. Place the pork chops on the hotter area of the grill and cover. Grill, turning occasionally, until the pork is seared with grill marks, about 5 minutes. Move the pork to the cooler area of the grill and continue grilling, turning occasionally, until the pork feels almost firm with some spring when pressed in the meaty center, 10 to 12 minutes. (Pork chops, even thick ones, are often too thin to test with an instant-read thermometer. If you want to try, insert the thermometer horizontally through the side of a chop, allowing the tip of the thermometer to reach the center of the chop. It should read about 145°F.) During the last 5 minutes, toss the apricots with the oil in a small bowl. Place the apricots on the hotter area of the grill and cook, turning once, until seared with grill marks, about 4 minutes. Transfer the pork and apricots to a carving board and let stand for 5 minutes.

4. Pour the reserved marinade, including the garlic and ginger, through a wire sieve into a small saucepan. Bring to a boil over high heat. Reduce the heat to medium-low. Whisk in the dissolved cornstarch and cook until thickened, about 15 seconds.

5. Serve the pork and apricots hot, with the sauce spooned over the top.

Roast Rack of Lamb with Mint Béarnaise

Makes 4 to 6 servings

The tradition of spring lamb is a British one. One popular breed lambed in the fall and the kids grew large enough to eat by spring. Combine this timing with the symbol of a lamb that appears often in Christianity, and you have lamb for Easter dinner. Rack of lamb is one of the most elegant of main courses, no matter what the season, but a fresh mint béarnaise sauce ties it into spring. The sauce need not be hot, as the heat of the meat will warm it sufficiently.

LAMB

Two 8-rib racks of lamb, trimmed,
    bones Frenched and chine bone removed

2 teaspoons kosher salt

½ teaspoon freshly ground black pepper

2 tablespoons olive oil, divided

¼ cup minced shallots

3 tablespoons Dijon mustard

1 garlic clove, minced

⅔ cup fresh bread crumbs

HERB BÉARNAISE SAUCE

¼ cup white wine vinegar

¼ cup dry white wine, such as Pinot Grigio

¼ cup minced shallots

3 tablespoons finely chopped fresh mint

1 cup (2 sticks) unsalted butter, cut up

4 large egg yolks, at room temperature

Kosher salt

Freshly ground black pepper

1. To roast the lamb, position a rack in the lower third of the oven and preheat the oven to 400°F.

2. Season the lamb with the salt and pepper. Let stand at room temperature for 30 minutes.

3. Heat 1 tablespoon of the oil in a large skillet over medium-high heat. One rack at a time, add the lamb to the skillet, meatiest side down, and cook, turning occasionally, until browned on all sides, including the ends, about 5 minutes. Transfer to a rimmed baking sheet. Stand the two racks on their meaty ends, interweaving the rib bones to stabilize the racks. Mix the shallots, mustard, and garlic. Spread the mustard mixture evenly over the top of the racks and sprinkle with the bread crumbs, gently pressing to help the crumbs adhere. Drizzle the crumbs with the remaining tablespoon of oil.

4. Bake until an instant-read thermometer inserted in the center of the lamb reads 125°F for medium-rare lamb, 15 to 20 minutes. Transfer the racks to a serving platter and tent with aluminum foil to keep warm. Let stand for 10 minutes while making the sauce.

5. To make the sauce, combine the vinegar, wine, shallots, and mint together in a small saucepan. Bring to a boil over high heat and cook until the liquid has reduced to about 2 tablespoons, about 5 minutes. Strain through a wire sieve into a food

processor or blender, pressing hard on the mint mixture with a rubber spatula. Reserve the mint mixture in the sieve. (If you leave the mint-shallot solids in the reduced vinegar, they will be pureed into the sauce and make it too thick. To add a bit of extra flavor and texture, the solids are returned to the finished sauce.)

6. Bring the butter to a boil in a medium saucepan over medium heat, then cook for 1 minute, taking care not to brown the butter. Pour the butter into a glass measuring cup. Let stand 1 minute, then skim off the foam on the surface of the butter. Add the egg yolks to the food processor. With the food processor running, slowly add the hot melted butter through the feed tube (or hole in the blender lid), leaving the milky white solids in the bottom of the measuring cup. Turn off the food processor and add the mint mixture to the sauce. Pulse the food processor once or twice to combine the sauce and mint solids. Season with salt and pepper to taste. (The sauce can be made up to 1 hour ahead. Transfer to a heatproof bowl and let stand in a skillet of very warm, but not hot or simmering, water. Or transfer the sauce to a wide-mouth Thermos.) Transfer to a serving bowl.

7. Cut the lamb between the rib bones and serve, with the sauce passed on the side.

An Easter Dinner

Asparagus and Spinach Soup with Mascarpone (page 32)

Roast Rack of Lamb with Mint Béarnaise (page 63)

Potato and Green Garlic Gratin (page 119)

Ragout of Spring Vegetables (page 117)

Coconut Tres Leches Cake (page 142)

Chicken Breast and Baby Artichoke Fricassee

This homey casserole is the kind of dish that one might find at a French bistro—tender chicken in a lovely wine sauce, perfect for spooning over egg noodles or rice. Do not be daunted by the instructions for cleaning the artichokes. Once you get the hang of it, this easy chore goes very quickly. For a side dish, serve steamed baby carrots tossed with butter.

1 lemon, cut in half

9 baby artichokes (1 pound)

2 tablespoons olive oil

2 ounces (⅛-inch-thick) prosciutto, diced

4 chicken breast halves, with skin and bone, about 12 ounces each

Salt and freshly ground black pepper

½ cup plus 1 tablespoon all-purpose flour

1 medium onion, finely chopped

2 garlic cloves, finely chopped

½ cup dry white wine, such as Pinot Grigio

1 cup canned low-sodium chicken broth

2 teaspoons chopped fresh rosemary, tarragon,
    or parsley, plus fresh sprigs for garnish (optional)

1. To prepare the artichokes, squeeze the lemon into a medium bowl and add 1 quart cold water. Working with 1 artichoke at a time, remove the first layer of dark green outer leaves to reveal the tender, pale green inner leaves. Using a paring knife, pare

away the dark green peel from the stem, and trim off the tip of the stem. Cut off the top third of the artichoke. Cut the artichoke in half. Using the tip of the knife, dig out the fuzzy choke. Place the artichoke in the lemon water.

2. Position an oven rack in the center of the oven and preheat the oven to 350°F.

3. Heat 1 tablespoon of the oil in a large ovenproof skillet over medium heat. Add the prosciutto and cook, stirring often, until lightly browned, about 2 minutes. Using a slotted spoon, transfer the prosciutto to a plate.

4. Increase the heat to medium-high. Season the chicken breasts with the salt and pepper. Spread the flour in a shallow dish. Coat the chicken with the flour, shaking off the excess flour. Place the breasts, skin sides down, in the skillet and cook until the skin is golden brown, about 3 minutes. Turn and lightly brown the other sides, about 2 minutes more. Transfer to the plate.

5. Add the remaining tablespoon of oil to the skillet. Add the onion and cook until softened, about 2 minutes. Stir in the garlic and cook until fragrant, about 1 minute. Drain the artichokes and add to the skillet. Pour in $\frac{1}{2}$ cup cold water and cover tightly. Reduce the heat to medium and cook until the artichokes begin to soften, about 5 minutes. Stir in the wine and bring to a boil, scraping up the browned bits in the bottom and sides of the skillet. Stir in the broth and reserved prosciutto and bring to a boil. Return the chicken breasts, skin side up, to the skillet.

6. Bake until an instant-read thermometer inserted in the chicken reads 170°F, about 30 minutes. Using a slotted spoon, transfer the chicken and artichokes to a platter and tent with aluminum foil to keep warm.

7. Let the cooking liquid stand, off the heat, for a few minutes, then use a spoon to skim off as much clear yellow fat from the surface as you can. Add the rosemary and bring to a boil over medium heat, stirring often. Cook until the sauce is lightly thickened, about 3 minutes. Season with salt and pepper and pour over the chicken and artichokes. Serve hot, garnished with fresh rosemary sprigs, if desired.

Duck Breasts with Rhubarb-Cherry Chutney

Makes 4 servings

The meaty, rich flavor of duck is well matched by a sweet-tangy chutney. Tart rhubarb makes a good chutney, but be forewarned that while it is tasty, it breaks down into a puree when cooked. Cherries add texture, color, and their own fruity flavor. I use dried cherries instead of fresh here, because local rhubarb and cherries may not be available in the produce markets at the same time. You will have leftover chutney, but it's great to have on hand for other meals—try it with grilled pork chops. The Couscous Salad with Radishes and Peas on page 42 would be the perfect side dish.

RHUBARB-CHERRY CHUTNEY

1 pound trimmed rhubarb stalks, cut into ½-inch-thick slices

¾ cup packed dark brown sugar

½ cup dried tart cherries

½ cup minced onion

¼ cup cider vinegar

¼ cup minced crystallized ginger

One 3-inch piece of cinnamon stick

½ teaspoon dry mustard

¼ teaspoon crushed hot red pepper flakes

1 garlic clove, minced

Duck Breasts

Two 14-ounce boneless duck breasts (see Note)

¾ teaspoon Asian five-spice powder

½ teaspoon kosher salt

⅛ teaspoon freshly ground black pepper

1. To make the chutney, combine all the ingredients in a medium nonreactive saucepan. Bring to a boil over medium heat, stirring to dissolve the brown sugar. Reduce the heat to medium-low and simmer, stirring occasionally, until the rhubarb is tender, about 7 minutes. Transfer to a bowl and let cool completely. (The chutney can be prepared, cooled, covered, and refrigerated, up to 5 days ahead.)

2. For the duck breasts, position a rack in the center of the oven and preheat the oven to 450°F.

3. Use a sharp knife to score the duck breast skin in a crisscross pattern, taking care not to cut through the skin to the flesh. Combine the five-spice powder, salt, and pepper, and use the spice mixture to season the breasts. Place the breasts, skin side down, in a large nonstick ovenproof skillet. Place the skillet over medium heat and cook until the skin is a rich golden brown, about 12 minutes. Pour off the fat in the skillet. Turn and cook until the meaty sides are browned, about 3 minutes.

4. Transfer the skillet to the oven and bake until an instant-read thermometer inserted horizontally into the center of a breast reads 125°F, about 5 minutes. Transfer the breasts to a carving board and let stand 3 to 5 minutes.

5. Using a large sharp knife, carve each duck breast on the diagonal into ¼-inch-thick slices. Slide the knife under half the slices from one breast, transfer to a dinner plate, and fan out the slices on the plate. Repeat with the remaining sliced breasts. Serve hot with the chutney.

Note: *The most common duck breasts (sometimes called magrets), from the Moulard duck breed, are quite large, so each yields two servings. Some supermarkets carry small Pekin duck breasts, about 7 ounces each. If using the smaller breasts, cook them in the skillet as described above to 125°F, but skip the final baking.*

Halibut with Sorrel Sauce

You won't find sorrel greens in many salads—-they are much too puckery for that. But when they are blanched, their lemony flavor is softened and they can be transformed into an elegant sauce for fish. This simple recipe is inspired by the French restaurant classic, and it is a perfect choice for a sophisticated main course at a dinner with close friends.

SORREL SAUCE

12 ounces sorrel leaves, tough stems removed, well rinsed (3 packed cups)

1 tablespoon plus 1 teaspoon unsalted butter

2 tablespoons minced shallots

¼ cup dry white wine, such as Pinot Grigio, or dry vermouth

½ cup heavy cream

Salt and freshly ground white or black pepper

HALIBUT

Unsalted butter for the pan

4 skinless halibut or turbot fillets, about 6 ounces each

½ cup dry white wine, such as Pinot Grigio, or dry vermouth

Salt and freshly ground black pepper

1. To make the sauce, bring a medium saucepan of lightly salted water to a boil over high heat. Add the sorrel and cook just until wilted, about 30 seconds. Drain in a wire sieve and rinse under cold running water. A handful at a time, squeeze the excess liquid from the sorrel. Chop the sorrel and set aside.

2. Heat the 1 tablespoon of the butter in a heavy-bottomed, nonreactive medium saucepan over medium-low heat. Add the shallots and cover. Cook, stirring often, until tender, about 3 minutes. Add the wine, increase the heat to high, and boil until the wine is reduced to about 1 tablespoon, about 2 minutes. Stir in the cream and sorrel and bring to a boil. Reduce the heat to medium and simmer, stirring occasionally, until lightly thickened, about 2 minutes more. The sauce may seem on the thick side, but it will be thinned later. Set aside. (The sauce can be prepared up to 2 hours ahead, dotted with the remaining 1 teaspoon unsalted butter, and kept at room temperature.)

3. To prepare the halibut, position a rack in the center of the oven and preheat the oven to 350°F. Generously butter a 13 x 9-inch glass baking dish. Arrange the halibut in the dish, skin side down, and pour in the wine and 1 cup water. Season the halibut with salt and pepper to taste. Cover tightly with aluminum foil. Bake until the halibut is barely opaque when flaked in the thickest part with the tip of a knife, 15 to 20 minutes.

4. Just before serving, reheat the sorrel sauce over low heat, stirring often. Keep warm. Using a slotted spatula, transfer each halibut fillet to a dinner plate. Strain the halibut cooking liquid from the baking dish through a wire sieve into a glass measuring cup. Using a wooden spoon, stir enough of the cooking liquid (about 1/3 cup) into the sorrel sauce to nicely coat the spoon. Season with salt and pepper to taste. Spoon the sauce over the fish and serve hot.

Sorrel

French chefs love sorrel, a perennial plant that shows up spring after spring in garden beds. Its wrinkled leaves resemble spinach, but its taste is surprisingly sour. In fact, it is so tart that it is rarely cooked alone as a side dish, and is instead incorporated into soups, sauces, and stuffings to impart a lemony flavor. Cream is usually a component in these dishes, as its richness balances the sorrel's pucker.

American cooks may also know sorrel as sour grass, which is a very appropriate nickname. Think of sorrel as a seasoning herb more than a vegetable and you'll be on the right track. The leaves are often blanched to mellow their flavor and will shrink quite a lot in the process. In the Caribbean, sorrel is something else altogether. The buds of the red hibiscus plant, also called sorrel, are steeped in hot water to make a bright scarlet beverage.

Salmon with Fresh Horseradish Crust

The eye-opening flavor of horseradish adds zest to these salmon fillets. This dish is almost embarrassingly easy to prepare—except for the fact that we can all use simple dishes that are special enough for company. And one thing that I have found about dinner guests is that they all love crisp, crunchy toppings like this one.

⅓ cup mayonnaise

¼ cup peeled and grated (use a microplaner) horseradish

2 teaspoons vegetable oil

Four 6-ounce skinless salmon fillets

Salt and freshly ground black pepper

8 teaspoons unflavored dried bread crumbs

Lemon wedges, for serving

1. Mix the mayonnaise and horseradish together in a small bowl. Cover and let stand at room temperature for at least 30 and up to 60 minutes to blend the flavors.

2. Position the broiler rack about 6 inches from the source of heat and preheat the broiler.

3. Heat the oil in a very large nonstick skillet over medium-high heat. Season the salmon with salt and pepper to taste. Place the salmon, skin side up, in the skillet. Cook until the underside is golden brown, about 3 minutes (or only 2 minutes if you like rare

salmon). Flip the salmon and cook for 1 minute. Remove from the heat. Spread each fillet with an equal amount of the mayonnaise mixture. Sprinkle each with 2 teaspoons of the bread crumbs.

4. Place the skillet with the salmon in the broiler and broil until the topping is browned and bubbling, about 2 minutes. Transfer each fillet to a dinner plate and serve hot, with the lemon wedges.

Asparagus, Ham, and Poached Eggs on Cheese Polenta

Here is a kind of Mediterranean eggs Benedict perfect for a springtime brunch—a sauté of asparagus and ham, served over a bowl of soft and creamy polenta, topped with a poached egg to act as a kind of sauce. When I was a chef, I poached countless eggs in my day, and I share my favorite make-ahead method. If you aren't fond of poached eggs, top each serving with a fried egg instead.

POACHED EGGS

1 tablespoon distilled white vinegar

6 large eggs

ASPARAGUS-HAM SAUTÉ

1 tablespoon unsalted butter

5 ounces smoked ham, cut into ½-inch dice

2 tablespoons minced shallots

1 pound asparagus, trimmed and cut into 1-inch lengths

2 tablespoons dry sherry

⅓ cup heavy cream

Salt and freshly ground black pepper

Cheese Polenta

2 cups milk

¾ teaspoon fine sea salt

1 ⅓ cups instant polenta

½ cup (2 ounces) freshly grated Parmesan

Chopped fresh chives, for garnish

1. To make the poached eggs, combine 2 quarts water and the vinegar in a large skillet. Bring to a boil over high heat. Reduce the heat to very low to maintain the water at a bare simmer. Place a bowl of hot tap water near the stove.

2. Crack an egg into a ramekin. With the ramekin close to the simmering water, pour the egg into the water. Using a large metal slotted spoon, quickly spoon the egg white back onto the remainder of the egg. Cook very gently until the egg white is opaque and the egg is just firm enough to hold its shape, 3 to 4 minutes. Using the slotted spoon, carefully transfer the poached egg to the bowl of hot water, trimming off any stray strands of egg white. Repeat with the remaining eggs. With practice, you should be able to poach three or four eggs at the same time, but keep track of the eggs so they don't overcook. The hot water will keep the eggs at serving temperature for up to 10 minutes. (The poached eggs can also be made up to 1 hour ahead. Use cold, not hot, water to hold the eggs. When ready to serve, bring fresh water without vinegar to a simmer in the skillet, then remove from the heat. Using a slotted spoon, transfer the eggs to the very hot water. Let stand just until warmed, about 1 minute.)

3. To make the asparagus-ham sauté, melt the butter in a large skillet over medium-high heat. Add the ham and cook until lightly browned, about 5 minutes. Stir in the shallots

and cook until softened, about 1 minute. Stir in the asparagus, then add the sherry and 2 tablespoons water. Cover and cook, stirring occasionally, until the asparagus is crisp-tender, about 5 minutes. During the last minute, add the heavy cream. Season with salt and pepper to taste. Remove from the heat and cover to keep warm.

4. Meanwhile, to make the cheese polenta, bring the milk, 2 cups water, and the salt to a boil in a medium saucepan over high heat. Whisk in the polenta. Reduce the heat to medium-low and let bubble, whisking often, until smooth and thick, about 2 minutes. Remove from the heat and stir in the Parmesan until melted.

5. Using a large spoon, spoon equal amounts of the polenta into warm serving bowls, making an indentation in the center of each mound of polenta. Spoon the asparagus-ham sauté around the indentation. One at a time, remove a poached egg from the water with a slotted spoon, drain well, and nestle in the indentation in the polenta. Sprinkle with the chives and serve hot.

A Springtime Brunch

Watercress Salad with Mangoes and Almonds (page 40)

Mango-Ginger Mojitos (page 20)

Asparagus, Ham, and Poached Eggs on Cheese Polenta (page 80)

Strawberry Mousse (page 160)

PASTA AND RISOTTO

Fettuccine with Fiddleheads and Ham

Lamb and Mint Risotto

Farfalle with Asparagus, Fresh Ricotta, and Chives

Fettuccine with Garlic Scape Pesto

Pasta Primavera Carbonara

Asian Rice Noodles with Beef and Pea Shoots

Thai Fried Rice with Shrimp and Sugar Snap Peas

Fettuccine with Fiddleheads and Ham

Makes 4 servings

The earthy flavors of fiddleheads and mushrooms are a perfect match. Combined with tender fettuccine and nuggets of smoked ham in a creamy sauce, this is a reminder that pasta is often at its best when served in small portions for a first course. The only trick here (and it isn't a hard one) is to cook the pasta and sauce so they are done at about the same time.

Salt

8 ounces fiddleheads, trimmed and cleaned

1 pound fettuccine

2 tablespoons unsalted butter

8 ounces smoked ham, cut into bite-sized pieces

8 ounces cremini mushrooms, sliced

¾ cup heavy cream

Salt and freshly ground black pepper

½ cup freshly grated Parmesan, plus more for serving

Chopped fresh chives, for serving

1. Bring a medium saucepan of lightly salted water to a boil over high heat. Add the fiddleheads and cook just until crisp-tender, about 3 minutes. Drain, rinse under cold running water, and rinse again. Set aside.

2. Bring a large pot of lightly salted water to a boil over high heat. Add the pasta and cook according to the package instructions until al dente.

3. Meanwhile, melt the butter in a large skillet over medium-high heat. Add the ham and cook, stirring occasionally, until it is beginning to brown, about 3 minutes. Add the cremini and cook, stirring occasionally, until they give off their juices, about 3 minutes longer. Stir in the fiddleheads and cream and bring to a boil. Season with salt and pepper to taste. Remove from the heat and cover to keep warm.

4. Drain the pasta and return to the pot. Add the sauce and Parmesan, season with salt and pepper, and mix well. Serve hot, sprinkled with chives, and with additional Parmesan passed on the side.

Fiddleheads

For just a few weeks every spring, fiddleheads make a brief appearance at farmers' and produce markets. They get their name from their shape, which looks just like the scroll of a violin.

Fiddleheads are young fern shoots, which emerge from the ground tightly curled and unfurl as the plant grows. Foraged from wild ferns, they can be found for sale most readily in the northeast and northwest corners of the country. Happily, they are becoming more common elsewhere, but since they are from the wild and not cultivated, they can be pricey. Fiddleheads have a flavor that resembles asparagus, only earthier. If you can't find fiddleheads, you can substitute freshly cut asparagus spears.

Before cooking fiddleheads, rub them between your hands to dislodge and remove any flaky, dark brown skin. Cook them briefly in lightly salted boiling water to set their color. Be careful not to overcook fiddleheads, or they will get slimy!

Lamb and Mint Risotto

Makes 4 generous main-course or 6 first-course servings

When a chilly spring evening calls for a hearty, warming main course, consider this risotto. The traditional method does require almost constant stirring, but I don't mind that chore at all because it allows me to slow down and enjoy the pleasures of cooking.

7 cups chicken stock, preferably homemade, or canned low-sodium broth, with additional as needed

3 tablespoons extra virgin olive oil, divided

1 pound boneless leg of lamb, trimmed and cut into bite-sized pieces

Salt and freshly ground black pepper

1 medium onion, chopped

2 garlic cloves, finely chopped

2 tablespoons unsalted butter

2 cups rice for risotto, such as Arborio, Carnaroli, or Vialone Nano

½ cup dry red wine, such as Shiraz

1 teaspoon tomato paste

½ cup freshly grated Romano or Parmesan, plus more for serving

2 tablespoons chopped fresh mint

1. Bring the stock to a simmer in a medium saucepan over high heat. Reduce the heat to very low to keep the stock hot.

2. Heat 2 tablespoons of the oil in a large, heavy-bottomed flameproof casserole over medium-high heat. Season the lamb with salt and pepper. In batches, add the lamb to the casserole and cook, stirring occasionally, until browned on all sides, about 3 minutes. Using a slotted spoon, transfer the lamb to a plate.

3. Add the remaining 1 tablespoon oil to the casserole and heat. Add the onion and cook, stirring occasionally, until softened, about 3 minutes. Stir in the garlic and cook until fragrant, about 1 minute. Add the butter and let it melt. Add the rice and cook, stirring often, until it is well coated with the fat and feels heavier in the spoon, about 2 minutes.

4. Add the red wine and the tomato paste to the rice. Cook, stirring to dissolve the tomato paste, until the wine is almost completely evaporated, about 1 minute. Add 1 cup of the hot stock to the rice and reduce the heat to medium-low. Cook, stirring almost constantly and adjusting the heat as needed to keep the stock at a steady, somewhat brisk simmer, until the rice has almost completely absorbed it, 2 to 3 minutes. Continue adding the stock, 1 cup at a time, stirring until it is almost absorbed, until the rice is barely tender and you have used all the stock, about 20 minutes longer. Add the lamb with the final batch of stock. The consistency should be loose, like a very thick soup, so stir in more liquid as needed. Add the butter, then stir in the rice, red wine, and tomato paste.

5. Remove from the heat and stir in the Romano and mint. Season with salt and pepper to taste.

6. Spoon into bowls and serve immediately, with more grated cheese passed on the side.

Farfalle with Asparagus, Fresh Ricotta, and Chives

Makes 4 to 6 servings

Of course, you can easily find commercial ricotta at the supermarket, but with a little more effort you can also get handmade fresh ricotta at an Italian delicatessen or cheese store. The latter is very perishable, with an incredibly creamy texture and a milky flavor that lends a special silkiness to dishes. While you are sure to enjoy this bow-tie pasta dish with regular ricotta, you will love it when made with the fresh kind.

> 2 tablespoons unsalted butter
>
> ¼ cup finely chopped shallots
>
> 1 garlic clove, minced
>
> 1 pint cherry or grape tomatoes, cut lengthwise in halves
>
> Salt and freshly ground black pepper
>
> 1 pound asparagus
>
> 1 pound farfalle (bow-tie pasta)
>
> 1 cup fresh or commercial ricotta
>
> ½ cup freshly grated Parmesan, plus more for serving
>
> 4 tablespoons chopped fresh chives, divided

1. Bring a large pot of lightly salted water to a boil. Meanwhile, melt the butter over medium heat in a large skillet. Add the shallots and garlic and cook, stirring

occasionally, until the shallots are tender, about 3 minutes. Add the cherry tomatoes and cook, stirring occasionally, until they are heated through, about 5 minutes. Remove from the heat and season with salt and pepper to taste.

2. Snap off and discard the woody stems from the asparagus. Cut off and reserve the asparagus tips. Cut the remaining spears into 1/2-inch lengths and set aside. Add the spears (not the tips) to the boiling water and cook until bright green, about 2 minutes. Add the tips and cook until the asparagus is crisp-tender, about 2 minutes more. Using a skimmer or a sieve, transfer the asparagus to a bowl. Do not place the asparagus in ice water or rinse under cold water. Keep the water in the pot boiling.

3. Add the pasta to the boiling water and cook according to the package instructions until al dente. During the last minute, return the asparagus to the pot. Scoop out and reserve 1 cup of the pasta cooking water. Drain the pasta.

4. Return the pasta and asparagus to the pot. Add the tomato mixture, ricotta, Parmesan, and 3 tablespoons of the chives. Toss gently, adding enough of the pasta cooking water to make a creamy sauce. Season with salt and pepper to taste.

5. Serve at once, with a sprinkling of the remaining chives and extra Parmesan passed on the side.

Fettuccine with Garlic Scape Pesto

One day in early June, I came back from my farmers' market with a tangle of green garlic scapes, and this dish was born. Garlic scapes are much less pungent than garlic bulbs, but they still provide plenty of mellow flavor. While this dish is excellent as is, I sometimes stir a cup or so of halved cherry tomatoes into the pasta to add a splash of contrasting color and a little acidity.

GARLIC SCAPE PESTO

2/3 cup plus 1 tablespoon extra virgin olive oil, divided

1 cup coarsely chopped garlic scapes

1/2 cup freshly grated Parmesan

3 tablespoons shelled and chopped pistachios

Salt and freshly ground black pepper

1 pound fettuccine

2 tablespoons unsalted butter, at room temperature

Salt and freshly ground black pepper

Freshly grated Parmesan, for serving

1. To make the pesto, heat 1 tablespoon of the oil over medium heat in a large skillet. Add the garlic scapes and cook, stirring occasionally, until they soften, about 3 minutes. Remove from the heat and let cool.

2. Combine the garlic scapes, Parmesan, and pistachios in a food processor fitted with the metal chopping blade. With the machine running, gradually add the remaining

²/₃ cup olive oil and process, stopping the machine to scrape down the sides of the bowl as needed, until the pesto is smooth. Season with salt and pepper to taste. Transfer to a bowl, cover tightly, and set aside for up to 2 hours at room temperature. (The pesto can be made up to 2 days ahead, refrigerated in a covered container. Let stand at room temperature for 1 hour before serving.) Stir well before using.

3. Bring a large pot of salted water to a boil over high heat. Add the fettuccine and cook according to the package instructions until al dente. Scoop out and reserve ½ cup of the pasta cooking water. Drain the pasta well.

4. Return the pasta to the pot. Add the pesto and butter. Toss, adding enough of the pasta cooking water to loosen the pesto and coat the pasta. Season with salt and pepper to taste.

5. Serve hot, with extra Parmesan passed on the side.

Green Garlic and Garlic Scapes

I never know what treasures I'm going to unearth at my farmers' market. Lately, new forms of garlic have become the seasonal stars of the springtime offerings, and one had better get there early in the day to buy them before they sell out.

Garlic is a member of the onion family. It grows underground, and we all know the familiar mature bulb and its pervasive flavor and aroma. As the garlic grows, the bulb sends a green tendril-like shoot up through the dirt. The long, curly shoots, called garlic scapes, must be cut off or the bulb won't mature. Farmers used to keep the scapes as their treat, but now they are harvested and sold to garlic lovers. Scapes have an herbaceous, mild garlic flavor. When lightly sautéed in a little oil or butter, their flavor blooms and their texture improves, too—they can be a little too tough to eat raw.

The same farmer who supplies mature garlic and garlic scapes is likely to sell green garlic as well. Also called baby or young garlic, these immature garlic bulbs look very much like scallions. Use green garlic just as you would scallions, chopping up both the white and green parts, or just one or the other, as you wish. These also have a garlic flavor that whispers instead of shouts. When they are in season, you may find yourself wanting to put garlic scapes and green garlic in just about everything you cook, especially potato and pasta dishes and salads, stopping just short of desserts.

Pasta Primavera Carbonara

Makes 4 to 6 main-course or 8 appetizer servings

When I first moved to New York, pasta primavera was the dish of the moment. It was served at every restaurant, from the glittering Le Cirque to the humble corner diner, but it quickly lost its luster. This recipe brings it back to its glory, but I do not want to hear any comments about its over-the-top, indulgent ingredients list!

4 ounces pancetta, cut into ¼-inch dice

2 teaspoons olive oil

1 garlic clove, minced

½ cup heavy cream

¼ teaspoon crushed hot red pepper flakes, plus more to taste

Salt

3 ounces trimmed sugar snap peas (1 cup)

3 ounces (½-inch cut) green beans (1 cup)

1 pound asparagus, woody stems discarded, cut into ½-inch lengths

1 pound fava beans, shelled (1¼ cups)

1 pound fettuccine, preferably fresh

3 large eggs, at room temperature

½ cup freshly ground Parmesan, plus more for serving

1 cup halved cherry or grape tomatoes

¼ cup thinly sliced packed fresh basil leaves

1. Cook the pancetta and oil together, stirring occasionally, in a large skillet over medium heat until the pancetta is browned, about 10 minutes. Using a slotted spoon, transfer

the pancetta to paper towels to drain. Add the garlic to the fat in the skillet and reduce the heat to medium-low. Cook, stirring often, just until softened, about 1 minute. Stir in the heavy cream and hot pepper flakes and bring to a simmer. Remove from the heat and cover, with the lid ajar, to keep warm.

2. Meanwhile, bring a medium pot of lightly salted water to a boil over high heat. Add the sugar snap peas and cook just until they turn bright green, about 2 minutes. Using a wire skimmer or a sieve, transfer them to a large bowl of ice water. Add the green beans to the boiling water and cook until they are crisp-tender, about 3 minutes. Using the skimmer, transfer them to the ice water. Repeat with the asparagus, cooking just until crisp-tender, about 3 minutes, and add to the ice water. Finally, add the fava beans, cook until tender, about 3 minutes, and add to the ice water. Drain the vegetables and set aside. (The cream mixture and the vegetables can be prepared and stored at room temperature up to 2 hours ahead. Reheat the cream mixture before using.)

3. Bring a large pot of salted water to a boil over high heat. Add the fettuccine and cook according to the package instructions until al dente. During the last minute, add the reserved vegetables. Drain well. Return the fettuccine and vegetables to the empty pot.

4. Beat the eggs in a large bowl. Gradually whisk in the warm cream mixture, then the Parmesan. Pour over the pasta and toss. Add the cherry tomatoes and basil and toss again. Season with salt and hot pepper flakes to taste.

5. Serve hot, with extra Parmesan passed on the side.

Asian Rice Noodles with Beef and Pea Shoots

Makes 4 servings

In spring, the produce stands in New York's Chinatown are piled high with pea shoots. This dish is a tasty way to feature them at their peak: a garlicky, gingery noodle stir-fry with sliced flank steak. Feel free to substitute thinly sliced boneless and skinless chicken breast for the flank steak, but cook it a little longer until it is opaque, about 2 minutes.

8 ounces wide dried rice noodles

12 ounces flank steak

3 tablespoons soy sauce, plus more for serving

3 teaspoons cornstarch

¼ teaspoon freshly ground black pepper

½ cup chicken stock, preferably homemade, or use canned low-sodium broth

2 tablespoons oyster sauce

½ teaspoon sugar

3 tablespoons vegetable oil, divided

2 tablespoons minced garlic

1 tablespoon peeled and minced fresh ginger

12 ounces (about 4 packed cups) pea shoots

1. Soak the noodles in a large bowl with hot tap water to cover until the noodles are softened but not soft (they should have the texture of rubber bands), 10 to 15 minutes.

2. Meanwhile, holding a thin knife at a 45-degree angle, cut the steak across the grain into thin slices. Cut the slices in half crosswise. Whisk 2 tablespoons of the soy sauce, 2 teaspoons of the cornstarch, and the pepper together in a medium bowl to dissolve the cornstarch. Add the beef and toss to coat. Set aside for 10 minutes.

3. Whisk the chicken stock, oyster sauce, and sugar with the remaining 1 tablespoon soy sauce and 1 teaspoon cornstarch to dissolve the cornstarch. Set aside. Drain the noodles.

4. Heat a wok or very large skillet over medium-high heat. Add 2 tablespoons of the vegetable oil and tilt to coat the inside of the wok with the oil. Remove the beef from its marinade, leaving any marinade behind in the bowl. Add to the wok and stir-fry until the beef loses its pink color, about 1½ minutes. Transfer to a platter.

5. Add the remaining 1 tablespoon oil to the wok and tilt the wok to coat the inside with the oil. Add the garlic and ginger and stir-fry until fragrant, about 15 seconds. Add the drained noodles and stir-fry until hot, about 1 minute. Return the beef to the wok and add the pea shoots. Stir the broth mixture well to recombine the ingredients and pour into the skillet. Stir-fry until the pea shoots have wilted and the sauce has thickened, about 1 minute. Serve hot.

Pea Shoots

Asian cooks have long known the culinary pleasures of pea shoots. In the spirit of not wasting anything that is edible, the leaves and shoots of the pea vine are harvested along with the pods. Both lend a gentle pea flavor to dishes, but only one is a harbinger of spring.

Pea leaves, usually from California snow pea crops, are shipped to Asian-American produce markets throughout the year. Their sturdy, pale green leaves bear a resemblance to Boston lettuce. Usually too tough to enjoy raw, they are often stir-fried with garlic and a splash of sesame oil.

Pea shoots are much more delicate and appear in local markets in midspring. With delicate curls poking through a cluster of pale green leaves, they look sprightly, young, and certainly spring-like. I love them in stir-fried noodle dishes, but if they are especially tender, try them in a salad. Use them the day you buy them, because they wilt easily.

Thai Fried Rice with Shrimp and Sugar Snap Peas

Makes 4 servings

You may want to get in the habit of making extra rice as a side dish so you have leftovers to turn into fried rice the next day. (Don't try to make fried rice with hot, freshly made rice—it clumps.) This fried rice was inspired by a dish I had at my neighborhood Thai restaurant and delivers the spicy-salty flavors of that cuisine. When adding the fresh herb at the end, feel free to use your favorite: I rarely cook with cilantro because it is not a favorite in my household.

2 tablespoons plus 1 teaspoon vegetable oil, divided

1 pound medium shrimp, peeled and deveined

2 large eggs, beaten

Salt and freshly ground black pepper

4 ounces (1 cup) sugar snap peas, trimmed

¼ cup chopped shallots

2 garlic cloves, minced

1 small hot fresh chile pepper, such as Thai or serrano, seeds and ribs removed, minced

3 cups cold cooked long-grain rice, preferably jasmine

2 tablespoons Asian fish sauce (nam pla or nuoc mam)

2 tablespoons soy sauce

3 tablespoons chopped fresh cilantro, Thai basil, or mint

1. Heat a wok or large skillet over medium-high heat. Add 1 tablespoon of the oil and tilt to coat the inside of the wok. Add the shrimp and stir-fry until they turn opaque, about 1½ minutes. Transfer to a plate.

2. Add the 1 teaspoon oil to the wok and heat. Beat the eggs with ¼ teaspoon salt and a few grinds of pepper. Pour into the wok and cook, stirring almost constantly with a wooden spatula, until the eggs are scrambled into very soft curds, about 30 seconds. Transfer to the plate.

3. Add the remaining 1 tablespoon oil to the wok and tilt to coat the inside. Add the sugar snap peas and stir-fry just until they turn bright green, about 30 seconds. Add the shallots, garlic, and chile and stir-fry until fragrant, about 30 seconds more. Add the rice and cook, stirring often, until heated through, about 2 minutes.

4. Mix the fish sauce and soy sauce together in a small bowl. Pour over the rice mixture and stir well. Spoon into bowls and sprinkle each serving with the cilantro. Serve hot.

SIDE DISHES

Roasted Vidalia Onions with Balsamic-Sage Glaze

Fresh Peas with Pancetta and Mint

Braised Baby Artichokes and Carrots

Ragout of Spring Vegetables

Potato and Green Garlic Gratin

Mango and Date Haroset

Irish Soda Bread

Roasted Vidalia Onions with Balsamic-Sage Glaze

Makes 4 to 6 servings

Vidalia onions aren't really sweet—they are just less sharp than traditional onions. In this recipe, roasting renders them truly sweet, and gives them a melting tenderness, too. To balance the sweetness, they are finished off with a balsamic vinegar glaze. Try them with roast chicken or as part of a mixed vegetable platter at a vegetarian meal.

3 tablespoons extra virgin olive oil

3 Vidalia onions

Salt and freshly ground black pepper

2 tablespoons unsalted butter

¼ cup balsamic vinegar

2 tablespoons light brown sugar

1½ teaspoons minced fresh sage

1. Position a rack in the center of the oven and preheat the oven to 425°F. Line a large rimmed baking sheet with aluminum foil and oil the foil.

2. Peel the onions, leaving the root end intact. Cut each onion lengthwise into 6 equal wedges. Arrange on the baking sheet, drizzle with the oil, and toss to coat the onions with the oil, keeping the onion layers intact. Season with salt and pepper to taste. Bake, turning the onions over after 20 minutes, until the onions are browned and tender, about 40 minutes.

3. Meanwhile, melt the butter in a small nonreactive saucepan over medium heat. Add the vinegar and brown sugar and bring to a boil, stirring to dissolve the sugar. Increase the heat to high and boil until reduced by half, about 2 minutes. Set the glaze aside.

4. Arrange the onions on a platter, drizzle with the balsamic glaze, and sprinkle with the sage. Serve hot, warm, or cooled to room temperature.

Fresh Peas with Pancetta and Mint

Makes 4 servings

I remember one springtime trip to Italy when our hosts' garden was overrun with peas. We sat and shelled them in the time-honored tradition, enjoying each other's company while we worked our way through the full bowl of pods. We improvised this dish, cooked in the Italian manner.

1 ounce pancetta, finely diced

1 teaspoon olive oil

1 tablespoon minced shallots

2 pounds peas in the pod, shelled (2 cups shelled peas)

¾ cup canned low-sodium chicken broth

1 tablespoon chopped fresh mint

Salt and freshly ground black pepper

1. Cook the pancetta and oil in a medium skillet over medium heat, stirring often, until the pancetta is browned. Using a slotted spoon, transfer the pancetta to paper towels to drain.

2. Add the shallots to the skillet and cook, stirring often, until softened, about 1 minute. Add the peas and stir well. Stir in the broth and bring to a simmer. Cover and cook until the peas are almost tender, about 5 minutes. Uncover and increase the heat to high. Cook until the broth is evaporated and the peas are tender, about 5 minutes more.

3. Remove from the heat. Stir in the mint. Season with salt and pepper to taste. Transfer to a serving bowl and serve immediately.

Braised Baby Artichokes and Carrots

In general, baby vegetables may be cute, but what minimal flavor they possess is underdeveloped. There are exceptions, specifically baby artichokes and true miniature carrots (not the baby-cut ones). Braised together in a flavorful blend of bitter and sweet, these are an excellent side dish to simply prepared roasts, such as the Easter lamb.

1 lemon, cut in half

9 baby artichokes

Salt

12 baby carrots, trimmed and peeled

1 tablespoon olive oil

1 medium onion, chopped

1 cup canned low-sodium chicken broth

Freshly ground black pepper

Chopped fresh parsley, for garnish

1. To prepare the artichokes, squeeze the lemon into a medium bowl and add 1 quart of cold water. Working with 1 artichoke at a time, remove the first layer of dark green outer leaves to reveal the tender, pale green inner leaves. Using a paring knife, pare away the dark green peel from the stem and trim off the tip of the stem. Cut off the top third of the artichoke. Cut the artichoke in half. Using the tip of the knife, dig out the fuzzy choke. Place the artichoke in the lemon water.

2. Bring a medium saucepan of lightly salted water to a boil over high heat. Add the carrots and cook until crisp-tender, about 5 minutes. Drain in a colander, rinse under cold water, and drain again. Set aside.

3. Heat the oil in a large skillet over medium heat. Add the onion and cook, stirring occasionally, until it turns translucent, about 4 minutes. Drain the artichokes, add to the skillet, and stir well. Add the broth and bring to a simmer. Reduce the heat to medium-low and cover. Simmer for 15 minutes. Add the carrots and set the lid ajar. Cook until the artichokes and carrots are tender and the broth is almost completely evaporated, about 5 minutes longer. Season with salt and pepper to taste.

4. Transfer to a serving dish, sprinkle with the parsley, and serve hot.

Ragout of Spring Vegetables

Green beans, sugar snap peas, and asparagus are simmered together in a light sauce to make a lovely side dish. Don't worry if the vegetables aren't al dente—they should be on the tender side. If you wish, add a scattering of chopped chives or tarragon, but I usually don't, letting the flavors of the vegetables take center stage.

1 tablespoon vegetable oil

1 tablespoon minced shallot

8 ounces thin asparagus, cut into 1-inch lengths

4 ounces thin green beans (haricots verts), trimmed

½ cup canned low-sodium chicken broth

6 ounces sugar snap peas, trimmed

1 tablespoon unsalted butter

Salt and freshly ground black pepper

1. Heat the oil in a large skillet over medium heat. Add the shallot and cook, stirring often, until softened, about 2 minutes. Add the asparagus and green beans and stir well. Add the broth and bring to a simmer. Reduce the heat to medium-low and cover. Simmer until the vegetables are crisp-tender, about 5 minutes.

2. Add the sugar snap peas and stir well. Cover again and continue cooking until the sugar snap peas are bright green and the asparagus and green beans are just tender, about 4 minutes more.

3. Remove the skillet from the heat. Add the butter and stir gently so that the butter melts and lightly thickens the stock. Season with salt and pepper to taste. Transfer to a serving dish and serve hot.

Potato and Green Garlic Gratin

Makes 8 servings

My friend the cookbook author and cooking teacher Sherri Castle buys her green garlic at the farmers' market in Carrboro, North Carolina. Here's my adaptation of a sumptuous gratin recipe that she so generously shared with me. The secret is steeping the green garlic tops in cream to draw out every bit of their delicate flavor. If you want to make this for Easter dinner and green garlic isn't available, simply substitute 4 scallions for the green garlic.

3 green garlic stalks

1 cup heavy cream

1 cup whole milk

Pinch of dried marjoram

Pinch of dried thyme

1 tablespoon unsalted butter, plus more for the baking dish

2 pounds Yukon gold potatoes

1 teaspoon kosher salt

½ teaspoon freshly ground black pepper

1½ cups (6 ounces) shredded Gruyère

2 tablespoons freshly grated Parmesan

1. Trim the root ends from the garlic stalks. Cut the white and pale green parts of the garlic stalks into ⅛-inch-thick rounds; you should have ½ cup. Coarsely chop the green tops.

2. Combine the chopped garlic tops, cream, milk, marjoram, and thyme in a medium saucepan. Bring to a simmer over medium heat. Remove from the heat and cover. Let stand for 30 minutes to steep the flavors. Strain through a fine-mesh sieve and discard the solids.

3. Position a rack in the center of the oven and preheat the oven to 375°F. Lightly butter a 9 x 13-inch baking dish.

4. Heat the butter in a medium skillet over medium-low heat. Add the sliced pale parts of the garlic and cover. Cook, stirring often, until tender but not browned, about 3 minutes. Remove from the heat.

5. Peel the potatoes and slice them very thinly with a mandoline or V-slicer (or use a food processor fitted with the thin slicing blade). Transfer them to a bowl and toss with the salt and pepper.

6. Spread one third of the potatoes in the baking dish and top with half of the cooked garlic and half of the Gruyère. Repeat. Top with the remaining potatoes. Pour the warm cream mixture evenly over the potatoes, then sprinkle with the Parmesan.

7. Bake, pressing the potatoes down into the cream mixture with the back of a large spoon every 15 minutes, until the potatoes are very tender and the top is golden brown, about 1 hour. Let stand for 5 minutes, then serve hot.

Mango and Date Haroset

Of course, you can't have Passover seder without haroset. If you aren't Jewish, you may not be familiar with this fruit-and-nut spread. But many of my friends and colleagues are, and this recipe comes from my buddy, celebrity chef Jeffrey Nathan. I like to serve it at springtime brunches as a spread for matzo, even when it isn't Passover.

½ cup walnut pieces

⅓ cup pecan halves

3 tablespoons sugar

1 teaspoon shredded and minced fresh ginger (use the large holes on a box grater)

2 ripe mangoes, peeled, seeded, and cut into ¼-inch dice

⅔ cup seedless red grapes, quartered

½ cup pitted dates, cut into ¼-inch dice

1 teaspoon ground cinnamon

½ cup sweet white wine, such as Riesling

2 teaspoons fresh lemon juice

Matzo, for serving

1. Roughly chop the walnuts and pecans in a food processor along with the sugar and ginger. Transfer the chopped nut mixture to a medium bowl.

2. Stir in the mangoes, grapes, dates, and cinnamon. Gently stir in the wine and lemon juice. Cover with plastic wrap and refrigerate to blend the flavors, about 2 hours. (The haroset can be made up to 1 day ahead.) Remove from the refrigerator 1 hour before serving.

3. Transfer to a serving bowl and serve with the matzo.

Irish Soda Bread

Makes 1 loaf, 6 servings

In many households, it isn't St. Patrick's Day without a loaf of Irish soda bread. But this great recipe is also delicious year-round as a simple accompaniment to a hearty supper or even an afternoon snack to go with your "cuppa" tea. For such an easy bread, there is a fair amount of controversy about how to make it properly: Irish bakers are especially firm on leaving out such Americanizations as caraway seed or currants. Here's how I make it—plain as can be, but all the better for being slathered with butter. For a real treat, use imported Irish butter, which has a lovely flavor.

2 cups cake flour (not self-rising)

1½ cups all-purpose flour

1 teaspoon baking soda

1 teaspoon sugar

1 teaspoon salt

4 tablespoons (½ stick) unsalted butter, chilled, thinly sliced

1¼ cups buttermilk, as needed

1. Position a rack in the center of the oven and preheat the oven to 450°F.

2. Sift the cake and all-purpose flours, baking soda, sugar, and salt together into a large bowl. Cut in the butter with a pastry blender until the mixture looks like coarse bread crumbs. Stir in enough of the buttermilk to make a soft, shaggy dough.

3. Turn the dough out onto a lightly floured work surface and knead a few times until the dough comes together. Shape the dough into a ball and place on an unfloured baking sheet. Cut a 4-inch-long cross, about $\frac{1}{4}$ inch deep, in the top of the dough.

4. Bake for 10 minutes. Reduce the oven temperature to 400°F. Continue baking until the bread is golden brown and sounds hollow when rapped on the bottom with your knuckles, about 30 minutes longer.

5. Let cool for 10 minutes. Using a serrated knife, cut into thick slices and serve warm.

DESSERTS

Key Lime Meringue Bars

Fresh Apricot Tart

Strawberry-Rhubarb Pie

Cream Cheese Pie Dough

Coconut Tres Leches Cake

Hamantaschen

Cherry-Almond Crumble

Strawberry-Rhubarb Cobbler with Cornmeal Topping

Honey Panna Cotta with Cherry Compote

Spiced Rice Pudding with Mangoes

Strawberry Mousse

Kentucky Derby Ice Cream Sundaes with Bourbon Pecan Sauce

Double Strawberry Pie

Key Lime Meringue Bars

When I come across a bag of Key limes at the market, they usually make their way into these tangy-sweet bars topped with a thick meringue layer. Any dessert with lots of meringue is a friend of mine, but the topping could pose a problem if you plan to transport the bars. In that case, simply leave it out and dust the tops of the baked bars with confectioners' sugar.

Unsalted butter, for the pan

1 cup all-purpose flour, plus more for the pan

1 pound Key limes or 6 Persian limes

¼ cup confectioners' sugar

⅛ teaspoon salt

8 tablespoons (1 stick) unsalted butter, cut up, at room temperature

One 14-ounce can sweetened condensed milk

4 large eggs, separated

⅛ teaspoon cream of tartar

6 tablespoons granulated sugar

1. Position a rack in the center of the oven and preheat the oven to 375°F. Lightly butter an 8-inch square baking pan. Line the bottom and two short sides of the pan with a 20-inch length of aluminum foil, preferably nonstick, folded lengthwise to fit the pan, to form a "sling." Fold the overhanging foil to make handles. Butter and flour the foil, even if it is nonstick, tapping out the excess flour.

2. Rinse and dry the limes. Grate 1 teaspoon of lime zest from a few limes; set aside. Juice the limes; you should have ½ cup. (Leftover juice can be covered and refrigerated for up to 2 days or frozen for up to 2 months.)

3. Put the flour, confectioners' sugar, and salt in a food processor fitted with the metal chopping blade and pulse once or twice to combine. Add the butter and pulse about 12 times until the mixture begins to clump together. Press the dough firmly and evenly in the pan and pierce in a few places with a fork. Bake until the crust is set and beginning to brown, 15 to 20 minutes. Remove from the oven.

4. Whisk the condensed milk, egg yolks, lime juice, and zest in a medium bowl until combined. Pour into the hot crust and return to the oven. Reduce the oven temperature to 350°F. Bake until the edges of the filling look slightly puffed, 15 to 20 minutes. Remove the pan from the oven. Return the oven temperature to 375°F.

5. Beat the egg whites in a very clean medium bowl with an electric mixer on low speed until foamy. Add the cream of tartar and beat on high speed until the whites form soft peaks. One tablespoon at a time, beat in the granulated sugar and beat just until the whites form stiff, shiny peaks. Spread the meringue over the hot filling, being sure that the meringue touches the sides of the pan, foil-lined or not. Return the pan to the oven and bake until the meringue is tinged with brown, about 8 minutes. Transfer to a wire cake rack and cool completely.

6. Lift up on the foil handles to remove the bars from the pan. Using a sharp, thin knife dipped in hot water, cut into 9 bars. Discard the foil and serve. (The bars can be made up to 2 days ahead, stored in an airtight container and refrigerated.)

Note:

Meringue topping will always shrink a little as it stands. However, when the weather is rainy or humid, the atmospheric moisture makes it weep and contract more quickly than usual. As insurance against this phenomenon, the addition of a cornstarch paste to the meringue helps soak up excess moisture, so it stays intact longer. So, in humid weather, just before making the meringue, sprinkle 2 teaspoons cornstarch over 3 tablespoons cold water in a small microwave-safe ramekin or custard cup. Microwave the mixture on medium power, stirring well every 5 seconds, until it is hot and thickened into a gummy paste, about 20 seconds. (Do not boil.) After the whites have been beaten to the stiff and glossy stage, add the paste and beat on high speed until it is evenly dispersed throughout the meringue.

Key Limes

By taste alone, you may not be able to tell the difference between the juice of Key limes and the typical supermarket (Persian) variety, although some say the Key lime is a bit more acidic. But looks are another matter. Key limes are pale, not dark green, and about the size of a large candy jawbreaker. When zested, the peel gives off a fragrant, floral aroma that really sets the Key lime apart. You will see bottled Key lime juice, which some cookbooks recommend if you can't find the fresh variety. This is ridiculous—these cooks would never suggest using bottled lemon juice, and Key lime juice has a similar bitter taste.

Key limes are not native to the Florida Keys, although they thrive there and became naturalized after their introduction. It wasn't long ago that Florida was the only place to find them, where they were grown in residential backyards and sold at citrus grove stands. They are now available nationwide at supermarkets during their peak season, which starts in April. Look for them in green

net bags, about thirty-five limes to the pound. Key limes are also called Mexican limes (as they are the most common variety in that country) or bartender limes (for their affinity for flavoring beverages), especially when purchasing trees from a nursery. Make your margaritas, daiquiris, and mojitos with fresh Key lime juice and you will become the most popular bartender in town. A couple of Key limes squeezed into iced tea make it a special treat.

There isn't much juice in each tiny Key lime—you will need to squeeze almost every one of the limes in a pound to get ½ cup juice. To dig deep into the hard, somewhat dry flesh, use a reamer with a pointed, not a rounded, end. Include some grated lime zest to add that special aroma, but don't overdo it. Key lime juice, mixed with zest, can be frozen in an airtight container for up to two months.

Fresh Apricot Tart

Makes 6 to 8 servings

I have only recently come to truly appreciate apricots. Growing up with an apricot tree in the backyard, I ate one apricot too many as a kid and took them off my list of favorite fruits. Now I find the late spring reemergence of ripe, flavorful apricots to be an annual pleasure, and I make this very simple tart (with no rolling or prebaking of the dough or peeling the fruit) as a showcase for them. The result will look and taste worthy of a French bakery.

TART DOUGH

Unsalted butter, for the pan

1 cup all-purpose flour

3 tablespoons granulated sugar

¼ teaspoon salt

6 tablespoons (¾ stick) unsalted butter, cut into ½-inch cubes, chilled

1 large egg yolk

FILLING

8 to 10 apricots

¼ cup turbinado or granulated sugar

1 tablespoon unsalted butter, cut into small cubes

1. Position a rack in the bottom third of the oven and preheat the oven to 400°F. Lightly butter a 9-inch tart pan with a removable bottom.

2. To make the tart dough, put the flour, sugar, and salt in a food processor fitted with the metal chopping blade and pulse to combine. Add the butter and pulse 12 to

15 times until the butter looks like coarse crumbs with some pea-sized pieces. With the machine running, add the yolk and process just until the dough is moistened—do not overprocess.

3. Transfer the dough to the tart pan. Press the dough firmly and evenly into the pan, being sure that it is not too thick where the bottom meets the sides of the pan (it should form as sharp a 90-degree angle as possible). Refrigerate while preparing the fruit.

4. Cut the apricots in half lengthwise, cutting through the indentation. Remove the apricot pits and cut the apricots into quarters. Arrange the apricots, cut sides up, in concentric circles in the pan. Sprinkle with the turbinado sugar and dot with the butter. Place the pan on a baking sheet.

5. Bake until the crust is deep golden brown, the apricots are tender and tinged black in a few spots, and the juices are thick and bubbling in the center, about 45 minutes. Transfer to a wire cake rack and cool for 15 minutes. Remove the sides of the pan and cool completely.

Strawberry-Rhubarb Pie

I know that there is a strawberry-rhubarb cobbler recipe in this book and that there is also a recipe for Double Strawberry Pie (page 164). But, at the risk of strawberry (or rhubarb) overkill, I cannot resist including this recipe for the pie that has become the centerpiece of an annual springtime ritual. Every May I make a couple of these beauties and invite our closest friends over for a pie-and-ice-cream social.

FILLING

3 cups rinsed, hulled, and quartered strawberries

3 cups (¼-inch-thick) sliced rhubarb

¾ cup packed dark brown sugar

½ cup granulated sugar

¼ cup instant tapioca, ground to a powder in a coffee grinder or electric blender

2 tablespoons (¼ stick) unsalted butter, thinly sliced

Grated zest of 1 lemon

Cream Cheese Pie Dough (page 141)

Vanilla ice cream, for serving

1. To make the filling, mix the strawberries, rhubarb, brown and granulated sugars, tapioca, butter, and lemon zest in a medium bowl. Set aside.

2. Roll out one disk of the dough on a lightly floured work surface into a 13-inch round, about ⅛ inch thick. Transfer to a 9-inch pie dish. Trim the dough to a ½-inch overhang.

Spread the fruit filling into the pie shell. Roll out the second disk of dough into another round the same size as the first. Center the round over the filling. Fold the edge of the top crust underneath the edge of the bottom crust. Pinch the crusts together, then flute the edge. Pierce a few slits in the center area of the top crust to allow steam to escape. Freeze, uncovered, for 20 to 30 minutes.

3. Position an oven rack in the bottom third of the oven and preheat the oven to 400°F.

4. Place the pie on a baking sheet. Bake for 15 minutes. Reduce the heat to 350°F. Continue baking until the dough is golden brown and the juices are bubbling through the slits, about 40 minutes longer. Transfer to a wire cake rack and let cool completely (this will take at least 4 hours, so time accordingly). Serve at room temperature with the ice cream.

Cream Cheese Pie Dough

Makes enough for 1 (9- to 10-inch) double or 2 single piecrusts

If you want to serve homemade pie with seasonal fruits but are nervous about your dough-making skills, you can now relax. Old-fashioned shortening dough requires skill (if not plain old guesswork) when it comes to adding the water. This dough is moistened with cream cheese, which contains just the right amount of liquid, eliminating the guesswork. The cheese's dairy fat contributes to the baked crust's tenderness and flavor, and though it does tend to brown a bit more quickly than traditional crust, it is really no matter—just tent the dough with aluminum foil during baking if needed. If you use this dough for the Double Strawberry Pie on page 164, you will only need one disk of dough, so freeze the remaining dough.

2 cups all-purpose flour

¼ teaspoon salt

10 tablespoons (1¼ sticks) unsalted butter, chilled, cut into tablespoons

6 ounces cream cheese (not low-fat), at room temperature, cut into ¾-inch pieces

1. Put the flour and salt in a food processor fitted with the metal chopping blade and pulse to combine them. Add the butter and cream cheese and pulse about 12 times, just until the dough begins to clump together (butter pieces will still be visible). Turn the dough out onto a very lightly floured work surface and gather it together.

2. Divide the dough into two disks and wrap each in plastic wrap. Refrigerate for at least 1 hour or up to 2 days. (If the dough is chilled until it is hard, let stand at room temperature for about 10 minutes before rolling out.) The dough can also be frozen, overwrapped with aluminum foil, for up to 1 month. Defrost overnight in the refrigerator before using.

Coconut Tres Leches Cake

Makes 12 servings

There is something about a coconut cake that says "Easter dessert." Maybe it reminds me of the cakes Mom used to make for the holiday, which were often baked in cute animal shapes and coated with fluffy coconut "fur." Tres leches cake, a classic of Latino cuisine, is moist and luscious with three milk products (although in this recipe, I am stretching it a bit with coconut milk instead of the traditional condensed milk), and a final topping of toasted coconut. This version is a sheet cake that will be served directly from its pan, so use an attractive baking dish if you will be bringing it to the table. If you want to dress it up, serve it with a compote of strawberries and orange segments.

CAKE

Unsalted butter, for the pan

1 cup all-purpose flour, plus more for the pan

1 teaspoon baking powder

¼ teaspoon salt

⅓ cup whole milk

1 teaspoon vanilla extract

1 teaspoon coconut extract (optional)

5 large eggs

¾ cup granulated sugar

SOAKING MIXTURE

One 14-ounce can coconut milk (not cream of coconut)

1 cup whole milk

½ cup confectioners' sugar

1 cup sweetened coconut flakes

1½ cups heavy cream

¼ cup confectioners' sugar

1 teaspoon vanilla extract

1. To make the cake, position a rack in the center of the oven and preheat the oven to 350°F. Lightly butter the inside of a 13 x 9-inch baking pan. Dust with flour and tap out the excess.

2. Sift the flour, baking powder, and salt together. Mix the milk, vanilla, and coconut extract, if using, together. Crack the eggs into the bowl of a heavy-duty standing mixer. Place the bowl in a larger bowl of hot tap water. Let stand, stirring often, until the eggs are warm, about 5 minutes. Add the sugar to the eggs.

3. Using the whisk attachment, beat the egg mixture on high speed until it is very pale and tripled in volume, about 5 minutes. Reduce the speed to low. In three additions, beat in the flour mixture, alternating with two equal additions of the milk mixture, and mix just until smooth, scraping down the sides of the bowl as needed. Spread evenly in the pan.

4. Bake until the top of the cake springs back when pressed in the center, about 30 minutes. Cool in the pan on a wire cake rack for 10 minutes.

5. To make the soaking mixture, whisk the coconut milk, whole milk, and confectioners' sugar together in a bowl. Pierce the cake all over with a meat fork. In two or three additions, pour the soaking milk mixture over the warm cake, letting the first addition

soak into the cake before adding another. Cool completely. Cover with plastic wrap and refrigerate until chilled, at least 2 hours. (The cake can be chilled up to 36 hours ahead.)

6. To make the topping, position a rack in the center of the oven and preheat the oven to 350°F. Spread the coconut on a rimmed baking sheet. Bake, stirring occasionally, until lightly toasted, about 10 minutes. Cool completely.

7. Whip the cream, confectioners' sugar, and vanilla in a chilled bowl with an electric mixer on high speed until stiff. Spread evenly over the chilled cake. Sprinkle with the coconut. Cut into wedges and serve chilled.

Hamantaschen

Makes about 3 dozen cookies

When I first moved to New York, my Upper West Side neighborhood bakeries had some items that I had never seen before. Hamantaschen, the tricornered cookie that appeared every spring during the Jewish holiday Purim, was one such treat. It quickly became a favorite, and here is the recipe that my friend Judy Epstein taught me. These cookies are filled with homemade apricot filling, but feel free to use store-bought fruit, poppy seed, or prune (lekvar) canned filling.

APRICOT FILLING

1 cup coarsely chopped dried apricots

¼ cup sugar

1 tablespoon fresh lemon juice

DOUGH

2 cups all-purpose flour

1 teaspoon baking powder

¼ teaspoon salt

¾ cup (1½ sticks) unsalted butter (see Note), at room temperature

⅓ cup sugar

1 large egg, at room temperature, beaten

2 tablespoons fresh orange juice

1. To make the filling, combine the apricots, sugar, lemon juice, and ⅓ cup water together in a heavy-bottomed medium saucepan. Bring to a simmer over medium heat. Cook, stirring occasionally, until the apricots are very tender and the liquid has evaporated,

about 10 minutes. Transfer the apricot mixture to a food processor and puree. Scrape into a bowl and cool completely.

2. Sift the flour, baking powder and salt together; set aside. Cream the butter and sugar together in a medium bowl with an electric mixer on high speed until light in color and texture, about 3 minutes. On low speed, beat in the flour mixture, then the egg and orange juice. Divide the dough in half and then shape into two thick disks. Cover in plastic wrap and refrigerate just until chilled, at least 1 and up to 3 hours. (The dough is easiest to work with if not chilled until hard. If it is too rigid, hit the dough firmly a few times with a rolling pin and let stand at room temperature for 5 to 10 minutes before rolling out.)

3. Position a rack in the center and top third of the oven and preheat the oven to 325°F. Line two baking sheets with parchment paper or silicone baking mats.

4. Place an unwrapped dough disk on a lightly floured work surface, dust the top with flour, and roll out $\frac{1}{8}$ inch thick. Do not roll the dough too thinly. Using a 2$\frac{3}{4}$-inch round cookie cutter, cut out rounds of dough. Gather up the scraps, press gently together, and refrigerate. Place a scant teaspoon of filling in the center of each round. Tightly pinch the dough at the top and both sides of each round to make a tricornered cookie with a small amount of the dough peeking through the center opening. Transfer to the baking sheets, spacing about 1 inch apart. Repeat with the remaining dough, including the scraps.

5. Bake, switching the positions of the baking sheets from top to bottom and front to back halfway through baking, until golden brown, 25 to 30 minutes. Let cool on the pans for 5 minutes, then transfer to wire cake racks and cool completely.

Note: *If you want to make these without dairy products, substitute regular (salted) margarine for the butter and delete the salt from the ingredients.*

Cherry-Almond Crumble

Makes 6 servings

The flavors of cherries and almonds are very complementary, as this homey
dessert with its crumbly topping shows. You'll need a good cherry pitter
to prepare the fruit. While the typical handheld pitter works fine, for large
amounts of cherries like this, I use a plastic plunger-style cherry pitter made
by Leifheit and available online and at well-stocked kitchen stores.

ALMOND CRUMBLE

½ cup sliced blanched almonds

½ cup granulated sugar

½ cup all-purpose flour

Pinch of salt

8 tablespoons (1 stick) unsalted butter, chilled, cut into tablespoons

½ teaspoon almond extract

CHERRY FILLING

2¾ pounds Bing cherries, pitted (7 cups)

½ cup packed light brown sugar

2 tablespoons cornstarch

2 tablespoons unsalted butter, diced, plus more for the pan

1 tablespoon fresh lemon juice

Vanilla ice cream, for serving

1. To make the almond crumble, process the almonds and sugar in a food processor
   fitted with the metal chopping blade until the almonds are ground into a powder.

Add the flour and salt and pulse until combined. Add the butter and pulse until the mixture is crumbly. Sprinkle with the almond extract and pulse two or three times to distribute the extract. Pour the mixture into a bowl and freeze for 15 minutes.

2. Position a rack in the center of the oven and preheat the oven to 375°F. Lightly butter a 13 x 9-inch baking pan.

3. To make the filling, combine the cherries, brown sugar, cornstarch, butter, and lemon juice in a large bowl. Let stand until the cherries begin to give off some juices, about 15 minutes. Transfer to the baking pan. Scatter the almond crumble over the cherry mixture.

4. Bake until the cherry mixture is bubbling and the topping is browned, about 35 minutes. Let cool until warm, about 20 minutes. Serve warm in bowls with the ice cream.

Strawberry-Rhubarb Cobbler with Cornmeal Topping

Makes 6 servings

For a couple of glorious weeks each spring, the farm stand near my town offers both homegrown strawberries and their very own rhubarb. This is a combination that most bakers can't resist, and I am no exception. The amount of fruit filling will seem like too much at first, but it will cook down, so don't skimp.

FILLING

3 pounds strawberries, hulled and cut in half (7 cups)

1¾ pounds rhubarb stalks, cut into ½-inch lengths (5 cups)

1⅓ cups packed light brown sugar

¼ cup cornstarch

4 tablespoons (½ stick) unsalted butter, chilled and thinly sliced, plus more for the pan

A few drops of red food coloring (optional)

TOPPING

1½ cups all-purpose flour

½ cup yellow cornmeal, preferably stone-ground

2 tablespoons granulated sugar

1 tablespoon baking powder

½ teaspoon baking soda

¼ teaspoon salt

8 tablespoons (1 stick) unsalted butter, thinly sliced

1 cup buttermilk, or more as needed

Vanilla ice cream, for serving

1. Position a rack in the center of the oven and preheat the oven to 400°F. Lightly butter a 3-quart baking dish.

2. To make the filling, combine the strawberries, rhubarb, brown sugar, cornstarch, butter, and food coloring, if using, in a large bowl. Transfer to the baking dish. Bake, stirring occasionally, until the mixture is juicy, about 20 minutes.

3. Meanwhile, make the topping. Sift the flour, cornmeal, sugar, baking powder, baking soda, and salt together into a large bowl. Add the butter. Using a pastry blender, cut in the butter until the mixture resembles coarse bread crumbs with some pea-sized pieces of butter. Stir in enough of the buttermilk to make a soft, but not wet, dough.

4. Turn out the dough onto a lightly floured surface and knead briefly to smooth out the dough. Pat the dough to a 1/2-inch thickness. Using a 2 3/4-inch round cookie cutter, cut out rounds. Gather up the scraps, pat out again, and cut out more rounds to make a total of 8 rounds.

5. Remove the baking dish from the oven. Arrange the dough rounds on the filling and return the dish to the oven. Bake until the rounds are golden brown, about 30 minutes.

6. Let cool 20 to 30 minutes. Serve warm in bowls with the ice cream.

Rhubarb

Is there anyone who would choose rhubarb as their favorite spring ingredient? It is tart to the point of rudeness. Yet I can't imagine the season without cooking at least one strawberry-rhubarb dessert or making a batch of gingery rhubarb chutney.

Rhubarb, actually a vegetable, just isn't very tasty by itself, so it is often combined with fruits (and plenty of sugar) to bring it up to snuff. There are recipes for pie and other dishes that use rhubarb alone, but they must be remnants of an earlier time when rhubarb was one of the first spring plants ready for consumption and people were desperate for fresh food.

Fresh rhubarb stalks are a lovely red-pink. Unfortunately, they turn pale and washed out when cooked. To replenish the rhubarb's crimson color, this is one of the very rare occasions where I would advocate the use of food coloring. Be judicious—you'll only need a drop or two.

Honey Panna Cotta with Cherry Compote

Makes 6 servings

Where I grew up, the first cherries arrive in June, so I still think of them as a late spring crop. You may have to wait a little longer for local cherries in your area, but when they arrive, this is a good recipe for showing them off. The plump fruit, barely cooked in its own juices, makes an excellent contrast to the smooth creaminess of panna cotta.

PANNA COTTA

Vegetable oil for the ramekins

2½ teaspoons unflavored gelatin powder

1 cup whole milk

2 cups heavy cream

½ cup mild honey, such as orange blossom

1 vanilla bean, split lengthwise

CHERRY COMPOTE

2 cups pitted Bing cherries

2 tablespoons sugar

1 tablespoon mild honey, such as orange blossom

1. Lightly coat the inside of six 6-ounce ramekins or custard cups with the vegetable oil. Sprinkle the gelatin over ¼ cup of the milk in a small bowl. Let stand until the gelatin softens, about 5 minutes.

2. Meanwhile, combine the cream, remaining ³/₄ cup milk, honey, and the vanilla bean in a heavy-bottomed medium saucepan. Heat over medium-low heat, stirring often, until small bubbles form around the edge of the cream mixture, about 5 minutes. Remove from the heat. Add the gelatin mixture and stir well until completely dissolved. Scrape the seeds from the vanilla bean into the cream mixture. Reserve the vanilla bean for another use or discard.

3. Carefully pour or ladle equal amounts of the cream mixture into ramekins. Refrigerate until the cream mixture is just cooled, about 1 hour. Cover each ramekin with plastic wrap and refrigerate until completely set, at least 4 hours and up to 2 days.

4. To make the compote, combine the cherries, sugar, and honey in a medium saucepan. Cook over medium heat, stirring occasionally, just until the mixture is juicy and the sugar dissolves, about 5 minutes. The cherries should retain their shape. Transfer to a bowl and let cool completely. (The compote can be prepared up to 1 day ahead, covered and refrigerated.)

5. To serve, uncover the ramekins. Working with one ramekin at a time, use your thumbs to gently press around the circumference of the set panna cotta mixture to release it from the sides of the ramekin. Invert onto a dessert plate. Holding the ramekin and plate together, give them a firm shake to unmold the panna cotta onto the plate. If it is stubborn, dip the ramekin (right side up) in a bowl of hot water and hold for 10 seconds, dry the ramekin, and invert again.

6. Spoon the compote and its juices over each panna cotta and serve chilled.

Spiced Rice Pudding with Mangoes

Makes 6 servings

There are countless ways to make rice pudding (my grandmother's was very custardy), but this slow-baked, egg-free version has its proponents. The sugar in the recipe interferes with the softening of the rice, so don't be surprised at the length of time needed for the grains to cook to tenderness. Medium-grain rice, such as Italian Arborio or Spanish Valencia (or any rice suitable for risotto or paella), will give off its starch and enrich the pudding. Fragrant mangoes add a splash of color and tropical flavor to this plebeian dish.

5 cups whole milk, plus more as needed

Three 3-inch cinnamon sticks

3 star anise

4 cardamom pods, coarsely crushed

⅓ cup medium-grain rice, such as Arborio or Valencia

⅓ cup sugar

1 tablespoon unsalted butter, plus more for the dish

1 teaspoon vanilla extract

2 ripe mangoes, pitted, peeled, and cut into ½-inch dice

1. Combine 4 cups of the milk, cinnamon, star anise, and cardamom in a medium saucepan. Bring to a simmer over medium heat. Remove from the heat and cover. Let stand for 30 minutes. Strain the milk mixture into a bowl, reserving the cinnamon and star anise but discarding the cardamom.

2. Meanwhile, position a rack in the center of the oven and preheat the oven to 300°F. Lightly butter an 8-inch square baking dish.

3. Pour the milk back into the saucepan, and return the cinnamon and star anise. Stir in the rice, sugar, and butter. Bring to a simmer, stirring often to dissolve the sugar. Pour into the baking dish.

4. Bake, stirring every 15 minutes, until the rice is very tender and the milk has reduced by about half, about $1\frac{1}{4}$ hours. Remove the dish from the oven. Stir in enough of the remaining milk to give the pudding a creamy consistency. Remove the cinnamon and star anise. Stir in the vanilla. Let cool until warm.

5. Sprinkle the mangoes over the pudding. Serve warm or refrigerate until chilled.

Strawberry Mousse

I was experimenting with a strawberry semifreddo, an ice-cream-like frozen confection, but thanks to the water in the fruit, the finished dessert was too icy for my taste. However, it was still delicious as a chilled (but not frozen) mousse.

MOUSSE

1 pound strawberries, leaves removed

1 tablespoon fresh lemon juice

4 large egg whites

⅔ cup granulated sugar

¾ cup heavy cream

1 teaspoon vanilla extract

STRAWBERRY SAUCE

8 ounces strawberries, leaves removed

2 tablespoons confectioners' sugar, or more to taste

2 teaspoons fresh lemon juice

1. To make the mousse, puree the strawberries and lemon juice in a food processor. Pour into a large bowl and refrigerate while making the rest of the recipe.

2. Combine the egg whites and sugar in the top part of a double boiler. Place over barely simmering water and whisk constantly until an instant-read thermometer reads 140°F, about 3 minutes. Remove from the heat. Beat with the whisk or an electric handheld mixer at high speed until stiff peaks form.

3. Whip the cream and vanilla in a chilled large bowl with the whisk or electric mixer just until stiff. Scrape the whipped cream over the strawberry puree, and use a rubber spatula to fold them together until almost combined but still streaky. Add the egg whites and fold them into the mixture until they are combined. Cover and refrigerate until chilled, at least 1 and up to 6 hours.

4. To make the sauce, puree the strawberries, confectioners' sugar, and lemon juice in a food processor. Pour into a bowl.

5. To serve, spoon layers of the mousse and sauce into six glass parfait glasses or dessert bowls. Serve chilled.

Kentucky Derby Ice Cream Sundaes with Bourbon Pecan Sauce

Makes 6 servings

Chocolate pecan pie is one of the classic Kentucky desserts. When I have friends over to watch the Kentucky Derby in May, I am likely to serve these delectable sundaes, which sport the same flavors of chocolate, nuts, bourbon, and caramel. To make serving easier, early in the day, scoop the ice cream onto a large rimmed baking sheet, cover with plastic wrap, and freeze. When ready to serve, freeze a serving bowl until chilled, then transfer the scooped ice cream to the bowl. You won't have to deal with the mess of last-minute scooping.

BOURBON PECAN SAUCE

1 cup pecans

1½ cups sugar

¼ cup light corn syrup

¾ cup heavy cream

8 tablespoons (1 stick) unsalted butter

3 tablespoons bourbon

½ teaspoon vanilla extract

1½ quarts chocolate ice cream

Whipped cream, for serving

Fresh mint sprigs, for garnish

1. To make the sauce, position a rack in the center of the oven and preheat the oven to 350°F. Spread the pecans on a rimmed baking sheet. Bake, stirring occasionally, until toasted, about 10 minutes. Transfer to a chopping board and cool completely. Coarsely chop the pecans.

2. Combine the sugar, corn syrup, and ⅓ cup water in a deep medium saucepan. Bring to a boil over high heat, stirring often to dissolve the sugar. Stop stirring and cook, occasionally swirling the saucepan by its handle and washing down any sugar crystals that form on the inside of the saucepan with a pastry brush dipped in cold water, until the mixture has cooked into a caramel syrup about the color of a copper penny. In addition to its color, the caramel will have a distinct toasted aroma.

3. While the caramel is cooking, heat the cream in a small saucepan or a microwave oven until hot. Carefully pour the hot cream into the caramel (the caramel will bubble furiously). Stir with a wooden spoon until completely dissolved. Remove from the heat. Add the butter and stir until melted into the sauce. Stir in the bourbon and vanilla. Add the pecans and stir well. Let stand until cooled. (The sauce can be made up to 1 day ahead, covered and stored at room temperature.)

4. To serve, scoop equal amounts of the ice cream into six dessert bowls. Top each with the sauce, then a dollop of whipped cream and a mint sprig. Serve immediately.

St. Patrick's Sundaes: *Substitute walnuts for the pecans, Irish whiskey for the bourbon, and vanilla for the chocolate ice cream.*

Double Strawberry Pie

More than a few bakeries have made their reputation on fresh strawberry pie when in fact the wonderful natural berries are glued together with artificial goo. This pie, adapted from a recipe by Paul Prudhomme, is bursting with real berries, through and through.

1 disk Cream Cheese Pie Dough (page 141)

3 pounds strawberries, rinsed and hulled

²/₃ cup sugar, as needed

1 tablespoon fresh lemon juice

A few drops of red food coloring (optional)

1 envelope unflavored granulated gelatin

Sweetened whipped cream, for serving

1. Roll out the dough on a lightly floured work surface into a 13-inch round, about ⅛ inch thick. Transfer the dough to a 9-inch pie pan. Trim the excess dough to a ½-inch overhang. Fold the dough under itself so the fold of the dough is flush with the edge of the pie pan. Freeze, uncovered, for 20 to 30 minutes.

2. Position a rack in the bottom third of the oven and preheat the oven to 400°F. Pierce the dough all over with a fork. Line the pie crust with aluminum foil and fill with pie weights or dried beans. Place the pie pan on a rimmed baking sheet. Bake until the dough looks set, about 15 minutes. Lift off the foil and weights and continue baking the crust until it is golden brown, about 10 minutes longer. Transfer the pan to a wire cake rack and cool completely.

3. Puree about 1 pound of the strawberries in a food processor or blender (you should have 1 1/2 cups of puree). Transfer to a bowl and stir in the sugar and lemon juice. Taste and add more sugar if needed. If desired, add red food coloring to heighten the red color. Set aside.

4. Sprinkle the gelatin over 1/4 cup cold water in a small bowl. Let stand until the gelatin softens, about 5 minutes. Place the bowl in a skillet of simmering water. Stir constantly with a small rubber spatula until the gelatin is completely dissolved, 1 to 2 minutes. Stir about 1/2 cup of the strawberry puree into the gelatin, then stir this mixture into the remaining strawberry puree.

5. Cut the remaining 2 pounds of strawberries into halves or quarters. Arrange the strawberries in a mound in the cooled pie shell. Slowly pour the strawberry puree all over the strawberries.

6. Refrigerate until the glaze in completely set, at least 1 and up to 8 hours. Cut into wedges. Serve chilled, with a dollop of whipped cream.

Index